9/13

Fourth Down
and
Inches

FOURTH DOWN

CONCUSSIONS AND FOOTBALL'S

AND INCHES
MAKE-OR-BREAK MOMENT

CARLA KILLOUGH McCLAFFERTY

CAROLRHODA BOOKS | MINNEAPOLIS

THIS BOOK IS DEDICATED TO THE MEMORY OF MY SON,
COREY ANDREW KILLOUGH MCCLAFFERTY

Carolrhoda Books
A division of Lerner Publishing Group, Inc.
241 First Avenue North
Minneapolis, MN 55401 U.S.A.

Website address: www.lernerbooks.com

Main body text set in Caecilia Com 10.5/16.
Typeface provided by Linotype AG.

Library of Congress Cataloging-in-Publication Data

McClafferty, Carla Killough, 1958–
    Fourth down and inches : concussions and football's make-or-break moment / by Carla Killough McClafferty.
        pages   cm
    Includes bibliographical references and index.
    ISBN 978–1–4677–1067–1 (lib. bdg. : alk. paper)
    ISBN 978–1–4677–1665–9 (eBook)
    1. Brain—Concussion. 2. Head—Wounds and injuries. 3. Football injuries. 4. Football players—Health and hygiene. I. Title.
RC394.C7M37 2013
617.4'81044—dc23   2013004192

Manufactured in the United States of America
1 – DP – 7/15/13

CONTENTS

PLAYING SPORTS

is my life...

I Live....

Eat....

Breathe...

and Dream

of the

Action....

the Excitement....

the Competition.

The wild

adventure of

each new GAME is

like walking on the

edge of

the HORIZON,

knowing

whatever is at the

END I will have

given to the game

EVERYTHING
I HAVE!

by Eric Pelly

"THE MOST CHERISHED OBJECT OF HIS LIFE"

VON GAMMON LAY DOWN ON THE GRASS AND TOLD HIS BROTHER TO STAND ON HIS HANDS. Von was strong, and he could prove it. Then he lifted his brother—all 6 feet 6 inches of him—clear off the ground. And Von wasn't just strong; he was skilled. When the guys gathered at the Gammon house, they could play almost any sport since his family had high jump and pole vault equipment, parallel bars, a punching bag, baseballs and gloves, tennis racquets, and footballs. Von was good at every sport.

When he left home to attend the University of Georgia, his friendly manner and good looks made him a favorite around the campus. His strength and athletic ability won him a spot on the football team.

On October 30 of Von's sophomore year, the Georgia Bulldogs were battling the University of Virginia. The Bulldogs trailed by seven points, and Virginia had the ball. Von took his place on the defensive line. The center snapped the ball. A mass of offensive linemen lurched toward Von, and he met them with equal force. The play ended in a stack of tangled bodies.

One by one, the Virginia players got up and walked away. Von didn't.

Teammates ran to Von, who looked dazed and couldn't speak. He was carried off the field. Two doctors looked him over and diagnosed a concussion. They called an ambulance to take him to the hospital.

Von was dead a few hours later.

Everyone was shocked and horrified to think Von died as a result of playing the game he loved so much. His loss made a lot of people wonder if football was too dangerous... too brutal... too violent. Some said football should be banned completely.

The *Atlanta Journal* ran a headline that read "DEATH KNELL OF FOOTBALL." It is a stunning headline, especially since the date was November 1, 1897.

| | | |

After Von's death, the University of Georgia disbanded its football team. So did Georgia Tech and Mercer University. A wave of anti-football feelings moved through the state, culminating in the Georgia state legislature passing a bill to ban football games. If Governor William Atkinson signed the bill, football would be outlawed in Georgia. It was a big decision, and since the bill was a direct result of Von Gammon's death, the governor considered the feelings of Von's mother, Rosalind Gammon.

She was very clear about how she felt. She did not want to ban football. She did not want Von's death to be used as a reason to ban the sport he loved. To her state representative, she wrote, "It would be inexpressibly sad to have the cause he held so dear injured by his sacrifice. Grant me the right to request that my boy's death should not be used to defeat the most cherished object of his life."

The governor vetoed the bill. Football would continue in Georgia and throughout the United States. And so would America's very complicated relationship with its most popular sport.

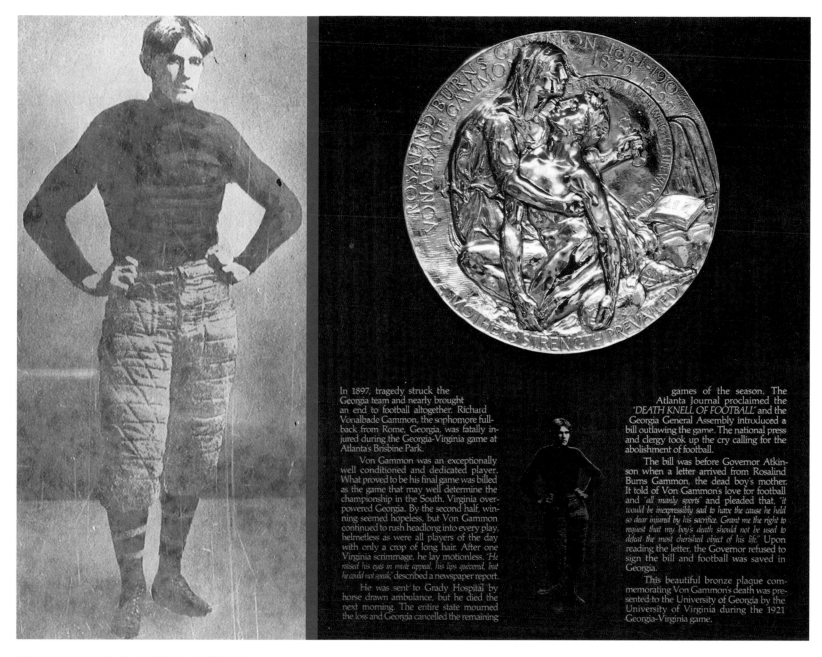

In 1897, tragedy struck the Georgia team and nearly brought an end to football altogether. Richard Vonalbade Gammon, the sophomore fullback from Rome, Georgia, was fatally injured during the Georgia-Virginia game at Atlanta's Brisbine Park.

Von Gammon was an exceptionally well conditioned and dedicated player. What proved to be his final game was billed as the game that may well determine the championship in the South. Virginia overpowered Georgia. By the second half, winning seemed hopeless, but Von Gammon continued to rush headlong into every play, helmetless as were all players of the day with only a crop of long hair. After one Virginia scrimmage, he lay motionless. "*He raised his eyes in mute appeal, his lips quivered, but he could not speak,*" described a newspaper report.

He was sent to Grady Hospital by horse drawn ambulance, but he died the next morning. The entire state mourned the loss and Georgia cancelled the remaining games of the season. The Atlanta Journal proclaimed the "*DEATH KNELL OF FOOTBALL*" and the Georgia General Assembly introduced a bill outlawing the game. The national press and clergy took up the cry calling for the abolishment of football.

The bill was before Governor Atkinson when a letter arrived from Rosalind Burns Gammon, the dead boy's mother. It told of Von Gammon's love for football and "*all manly sports*" and pleaded that, "*it would be inexpressibly sad to have the cause he held so dear injured by his sacrifice. Grant me the right to request that my boy's death should not be used to defeat the most cherished object of his life.*" Upon reading the letter, the Governor refused to sign the bill and football was saved in Georgia.

This beautiful bronze plaque commemorating Von Gammon's death was presented to the University of Georgia by the University of Virginia during the 1921 Georgia-Virginia game.

VON GAMMON IN HIS FOOTBALL UNIFORM

IN 1921, TWENTY-FOUR YEARS AFTER THE FOOTBALL GAME THAT COST VON GAMMON HIS LIFE, SURVIVING MEMBERS OF THE OPPOSING TEAM, THE UNIVERSITY OF VIRGINIA, DONATED THIS PLAQUE. IT WAS GIVEN IN HONOR OF VON AND HIS MOTHER, WHO IS SOMETIMES CALLED THE WOMAN WHO SAVED SOUTHERN FOOTBALL. THE PLAQUE SAYS: "MOTHER'S STRENGTH PREVAILED" AND "THE CAUSE SHALL LIVE IN WHICH HIS LIFE WAS GIVEN."

"THE MOST CHERISHED OBJECT OF HIS LIFE"

"BRAINS WILL ALWAYS WIN OVER MUSCLE"

THE GAME WAS ROUGH FROM THE BEGINNING. It started out as the British game of rugby. Then Walter Camp, an athlete at Yale University, changed the rules and transformed it into American football. Camp became known as the father of American football.

Young men loved the new game. Many were drawn to the sport's inevitable collisions, and Camp believed part of the attraction was the clash of physical strength. He said playing football was "the means of satisfying the instinct innate in every youth for a contest to demonstrate physical supremacy." He also believed mental strength was part of the appeal. Camp said, "It is not a test of muscle alone, for

THIS PHOTO SHOWS WALTER CAMP—FATHER OF AMERICAN FOOTBALL—AS THE CAPTAIN OF THE YALE FOOTBALL TEAM IN 1880. CAMP CHANGED THE RULES OF ENGLISH RUGBY TO CREATE A NEW GAME.

the greatest lesson of football may be expressed in a single line—it teaches that brains will always win over muscle."

Football spread from college to high school. Athletes knew playing the violent game was risky—which may have added to the exhilaration of it. The game was a perfect combination of brains, brawn, and brutality.

| | | |

In the early days of football, the rules were different in critical ways. Teams tried to gain five yards for a first down; they could not throw a forward pass; and they used what were called mass plays. This type of play involved

THE 1894 YALE FOOTBALL TEAM DEMONSTRATES THE FLYING WEDGE FORMATION.

the team moving together in one big group to overwhelm the defense with their momentum, sometimes gaining twenty yards in a single play. This style of play caused a lot of injuries because the big group of players would mow down the opponents, and when the whistle blew, both teams ended up in a pile of tangled bodies. These plays made it more difficult for spectators—and officials—to see what was happening with the ball because the players were bunched together.

Even though the game wasn't yet the perfect spectator sport, the passion and excitement of football wasn't only on the field. Emotions ran high in the stands. During the contest between Army and Navy in 1893, the tension was so great that a brigadier general and a rear admiral nearly fought a duel over the game. President Grover Cleveland called a cabinet meeting to discuss the situation. As a result, the departments of the Army and Navy decided the two military schools should not play football against each other in the future.

The next year on October 25, 1894, an article in the *New York Times* reminded its readers why the game between the rivals was banned. It said, "The rough character of the sport, combined with the fact that it distracts the attention of the cadets more than any other occupation, has operated to prohibit any games at the Military Academy or the Naval Academy."

Nevertheless, the Army-Navy game was reinstated in 1899 and has been played annually ever since. Through the years, the teams have played each other more than 113 times.

The Army-Navy matchup wasn't the only rivalry to cause emotions to run high. Harvard and Yale played an especially brutal game on November 24, 1894. During the game, the umpire caught two players "exchanging little fistic courtesies, and he promptly disqualified them." The game was considered to be too rough, and too much slugging took place. The injured players along with their injuries were listed in the *New York Times*:

Brewer, leg; Wrightington, collarbone broken; Murphy, concussion of the brain; Jerrems, head; Butterworth, head, Hallowell, nose broken.

FOOTBALL GAMES BETWEEN ARMY AND NAVY WERE BANNED FOR FIVE YEARS BETWEEN 1894 AND 1899 BECAUSE OF "THE ROUGH CHARACTER OF THE SPORT." WHEN THE GAMES RESUMED, THE TEAMS PLAYED IN THE NEUTRAL CITY OF PHILADELPHIA. THIS PHOTO SHOWS THE LARGE CROWD AT FRANKLIN FIELD DURING THE NOVEMBER 28, 1908, GAME. NOTICE THE FIELD IS MARKED WITH LINES GOING BOTH DIRECTIONS LIKE A CHECKERBOARD.

That 1894 Harvard-Yale game was so violent and resulted in so many injuries that it became known as the Hampden Park Blood Bath and sometimes as the Springfield Massacre. Consequently, the football games between the two rivals were canceled in 1895 and 1896.

After the two-year ban, the games between Harvard and Yale resumed, and so did their rivalry—now known as The Game. Some years as many as fifty thousand people watch the clash in the autumn.

THIS 1905 CLOSE-UP OF ARTHUR REUBER, TEAM CAPTAIN AT NORTHWESTERN UNIVERSITY, SHOWS THAT THE SHAPE OF FOOTBALLS THEN WERE ROUNDER THAN THOSE USED TODAY. NOTE, TOO, HIS RELATIVELY RUDIMENTARY PADDING.

"THERE SHALL BE NO STRIKING OF THE RUNNER IN THE FACE"

HARVARD WANTED TO BEAT YALE **ABOVE EVERY OTHER TEAM.** Hoping to help its chances, the school hired alumnus Bill Reid as head coach. Reid had been a great athlete during his student days, playing catcher on the baseball team that beat Yale three out of his four years on the team. Reid also scored two touchdowns to defeat Yale in the 1898 football game, which was only the third time Harvard defeated Yale since they began playing each other in 1875. Harvard quickly reverted to its losing ways, though, and didn't like it. The school was willing to do whatever it took to win again.

When twenty-six year old Reid arrived in March of 1905 to coach the Harvard football squad, he had one objective: beat Yale. And Harvard was willing to pay handsomely for him to meet that goal. It paid him the exorbitant sum of $7,000 a year, more than any other coach in America. The amount was more than any professor's salary at Harvard, and it was almost as much salary as the university president.

While Coach Reid prepared his Harvard football team for battle on the gridiron, Harvard University president Charles William Eliot prepared for a different sort of battle. Eliot was not a fan of football. The violence of the game made Eliot conclude that football was more brutal than boxing. He remarked that "the game sets up a wrong kind of hero—the man who uses his strength brutally, with a reckless

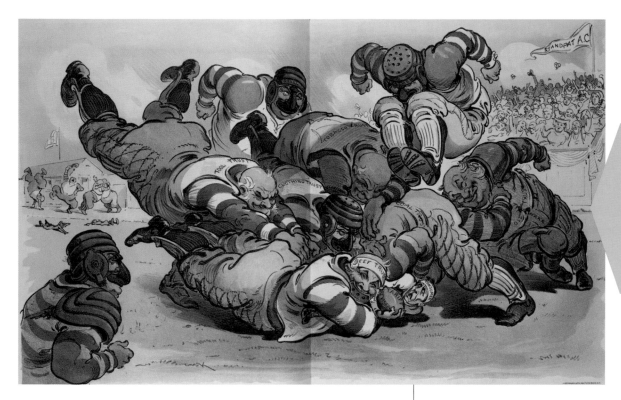

THIS CARTOON FROM 1905 ILLUSTRATES SOME OF THE BRUTALITY AND VIOLENCE THAT HAPPENED ON THE FOOTBALL FIELD. NOTICE THAT SOME PLAYERS HAVE HELMETS AND NOSE GUARDS WHILE OTHERS ARE BAREHEADED.

disregard both of the injuries he may suffer and of the injuries he may inflict on others."

Eliot was also concerned that many players were violating rules of fair play. Since mass plays like the flying wedge meant players were bunched up together, the umpires and spectators couldn't see illegal conduct. An article in the *New York Times* on November 30, 1905, wrote that Eliot "attacks the brutal instincts encouraged by improper coaching."

Eliot was not the only one who was concerned. Many Harvard University students believed the time had come for football to either change or be abolished. An article in the *Harvard Bulletin* said:

> There is something radically wrong with the game. It ought to be substantially changed or else abolished. We do not want the young men in the American colleges to play ladylike games or to give up any form of athletics because it may cause injuries. Rowing, baseball, lacrosse, association football [soccer] are strenuous enough, and have a moderate risk of injury, but no one objects to them. When, however, a game becomes so

"THERE SHALL BE NO STRIKING OF THE RUNNER IN THE FACE"

dangerous that several players are sure to be hurt in every contest between two teams it is time to admit that something is wrong.

Newspapers were filled with reports of football injuries and deaths during the 1905 football season. Many questioned what should be done. Should football continue as it was? Should the rules be changed? Should football be banned completely?

Opposing the game's critics were supporters who loved the game and believed it developed strength and courage among players. They accepted the risks. In an editorial in the *New York Times*, one man argued that any attempts to reform football would destroy it. He added that the game stimulated the "true ideal of manhood." He continued:

> When a boy runs down the field with the ball under his elbow and an opposition player tries to clutch him and he swings his arm around and cracks the other man's face, and permanently alters his nose and loosens up his ear, what does that teach him? It teaches him forbearance and patience. When he mixes in a scrimmage and finds it convenient to step on some other man's head in order to fling his weight on the wriggling pile of players, and

cracks a collarbone or two, and dislocated a wrist, what does that teach him? It teaches him humility and self-forgetfulness. And when a 225-pound guard takes advantage of the referee's inattention and smites the opposing player grievously with his doubled fist, and uproots his teeth and kicks him harshly in the ankle bone, and falls on him like a human pile driver, what does that teach him? It teaches him to be loyal and persevering and ever mindful of the rights of others.

The debate heated up. Meanwhile, football players continued to get hurt. Football players continued to die. And football players continued to love the game.

President Theodore Roosevelt knew where he stood on the matter. He supported football and football players. Although he never played the game himself, Roosevelt believed in living what he called a "strenuous life." He believed lessons learned on the football field prepared a man for the battles of life. In a letter on February 3, 1903, Roosevelt wrote: "It seems to me a good rule for life is one borrowed from the football field— don't flinch, don't foul, hit the line hard."

As the debates over football's brutality

gained momentum, Roosevelt gave a speech at the Harvard University Alumni meeting on June 28, 1905. He said:

> I believe in outdoor games, and I do not mind in the least that they are rough games, or that those who take part in them are occasionally injured…and I have a hearty contempt for him if he counts a broken arm or collarbone as of serious consequence when balanced against the chance of showing that he possesses hardihood, physical address, and courage.

Roosevelt's son Kermit was on the 1905 Harvard football team. The president wrote a letter to Kermit on White House stationery dated September 27, 1905. The president said Kermit's studies were most important but "it would be good for you to have the bodily development that comes from football."

Roosevelt personally wanted football to continue, but he also understood the public's growing concern over the brutality of the game as it was being played. As the number of football-related injuries and deaths grew during the 1905 season, even Roosevelt wondered if this would ultimately lead to the death of the game itself. Roosevelt had no problem with the fact that the game came with a risk of injury as long as the game was played fairly. And football's fairness was an open question to some. An article in the *New York Times* on October 15, 1905, said:

> There have been isolated instances of this recently, but for some years coaches have not instructed the practice of such tactics as they once undoubtedly did….However when it does crop up, as is once in a while the case, no penalty can be too severe to meet it, and permanent disqualification, not disqualification for a single game, should be inflicted.

The article said that for a gentleman "the unsportsmanlike spirit of wishing to win through an opponent's misfortunes had no place." Teddy Roosevelt believed that men who didn't play a "clean" game of football should receive the same punishment as a "man who cheats at cards or who strikes a foul blow in boxing." This was not to be tolerated. Roosevelt got personally involved. He invited the leading advisers and coaches of Harvard, Yale, and Princeton—the Big Three—to a meeting at the White House on October 9, 1905.

Roosevelt made clear what should be done: The brutality and foul play must stop. Umpires must be given the power to deal with problem

THIS CARTOON OF PRESIDENT ROOSEVELT HAS THE CAPTION, "NEXT! A PRESIDENT WHO 'DOES' THINGS." NOTICE THE FIGURE ON THE RIGHT IS A FOOTBALL PLAYER WITH A CRUTCH WHOSE JERSEY SAYS "BRUTALITY AND FOOTBALL." ROOSEVELT SITS ON A BUCKET THAT SAYS "COAL STRIKE" BECAUSE HE HAD BROUGHT TOGETHER THE TWO OPPOSING SIDES TO END THE PENNSYLVANIA MINERS STRIKE IN 1902. THE FIGURE ON THE LEFT SAYS "WAR" BECAUSE ROOSEVELT MEDIATED THE END OF THE RUSSO-JAPANESE WAR. ROOSEVELT WAS AWARDED THE NOBEL PEACE PRIZE FOR THIS IN 1906, MAKING HIM THE FIRST AMERICAN TO BE AWARDED A NOBEL PRIZE. FOOTBALL IS ON AN EQUAL FOOTING WITH WAR IN THIS IMAGE.

players. There must be an eligibility code that required all players be a college student and amateur sportsmen. And the rules of the game must be simple so as not to "offer too many loopholes." The president wanted the men from the Big Three schools to lead the way to reform the rules of football.

Harvard's Bill Reid wrote about this meeting with President Roosevelt in his coaching journal. He noted that Roosevelt discussed football in general and incidents of unfair play he remembered. Reid described the outcome of the meeting:

> At a meeting with the President of the United States, it was agreed that we consider an honorable obligation exists to carry out in letter and in spirit the rules of the game of football relating to roughness, holding and found play, and the active coaches of our Universities being present with us pledge themselves to so regard it, and to do their utmost to carry out these obligations.

Bill Reid and all the others signed the pledge, but implementing it was trickier.

To clarify what was meant by "roughness, holding and foul play" Reid attempted to spell it out. He suggested on rule 17C that there would be the following:

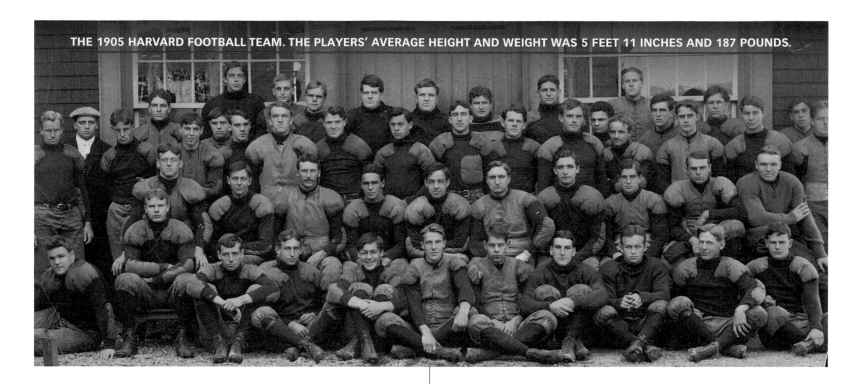

THE 1905 HARVARD FOOTBALL TEAM. THE PLAYERS' AVERAGE HEIGHT AND WEIGHT WAS 5 FEET 11 INCHES AND 187 POUNDS.

No use of open, palm extended or with clinched fists.... There shall be no striking of the runner in the face with the heel of the hand, in lieu of tackling.

For rule 27C, he said:

There shall be no unnecessary roughness, throttling, hacking or striking with the closed fist, we agree that there shall be no attempt in any way to injure another player, or to uppercut with the clinched fist the underbody of a player, or to make any intentional rough play with the elbows.

Reid submitted these suggestions to the coaches at Yale and Princeton.

Coach Jack Owsley at Yale wrote back, "As to the use of the hand or straight arm instead of tackling the runner, I regard that as necessary to prevent a man from successfully hurdling the line." Coach Art Hillebrand at Princeton wrote, "Your interpretation of rule 17C is not entirely satisfactory, and [I] would suggest a meeting to discuss it further." Even the coaches didn't see eye to eye on what should and should not be allowed.

While stakeholders were considering what adjustments to make, the 1905 football season continued.

"THERE SHALL BE NO STRIKING OF THE RUNNER IN THE FACE"

"MEND IT OR END IT"

THE WEEK BEFORE THE GAME BETWEEN YALE AND HARVARD, COACH REID'S TEAM HAD TO FACE DARTMOUTH ON NOVEMBER 18. Dan Hurley, from Charlestown, Massachusetts, was a first-year medical student and a halfback. He'd been chosen as captain of the team for the second year in a row—an honor not given to a captain for many years.

Hurley had been sidelined earlier in the season with a bad thigh injury. Then, during the Dartmouth game, Hurley, who was described as the "plucky little football captain," received a minor leg injury and a blow to the head. The following day, Reid wrote in his journal that "[team doctor] Nichols is afraid Hurley is a little out of his head." The coach also found out that during the Dartmouth game, his teammates said, "Hurley was blaming men for not being where they ought to be, when, as a matter of fact, they were doing just what they ought to do." At practice on Monday, Nichols told Reid to "watch Hurley very carefully and see if we could not discover something wrong with him, but we could not see how he was off at all, as to us he seemed perfectly rational." Later that Monday night, the doctor told Reid he didn't think Dan Hurley would be able to play in The Game.

On Tuesday night, the coach found out that Hurley went to the football ticket office where he asked for tickets—and crackers and milk. When the coach told Nichols, the doctor insisted that Hurly be accompanied wherever he went, "in order to prevent any possibility of accident through the chances of temporary insanity."

By Wednesday night, Nichols brought in a specialist to examine Dan Hurley and discover "what was the matter with his head." Reid wrote that the specialist "almost immediately announced that Hurley could not hope to play. What was more he would have to go right in town [to the hospital] and be kept quiet." At a student meeting later that night, Reid told a crowd of two thousand Harvard students that their team captain would not be able to play in the Yale game. Reid wrote in his journal that he "placed more emphasis on his leg than I did on his head. Since football is being severely criticized just at present, a case of concussion on the brain would be very serious."

Nonetheless, in 1905, articles about college football teams and players filled newspapers, especially since the violence of the game was becoming an unavoidable issue. The *New York Times* ran an article with the headline "Hurley Badly Injured." In it, Nichols explained that Hurley "is suffering from a serious injury to the surface of the brain which will prevent his entering the game Saturday." He said Hurley

had a blood clot on his brain and that he had symptoms that included an "unnatural irritability, and occasional incoherence in speech."

Hurley rested in his hospital bed with a low temperature and low pulse rate. But all he could think about was The Game. Two days before, he told his brother, "I'm going to play in that game if I have to jump through that window. To play against Yale this year has been the ambition of my life and there will be a fight if they don't let me out."

It didn't come to that. On game day, Captain Dan Hurley was unable to take the field. But his team hadn't forgotten him. The players cheered and sang songs for their teammate before the game, the Harvard students in the stands gave a cheer for their injured captain, and even Yale spectators applauded the absent Harvard man. Special equipment had been brought to Hurley's hospital room so he could be kept informed about what was happening on the field. The news wasn't good. Even though Harvard was coached by the well-paid Reid, they lost to Yale, 6–0.

A Harvard professor in the stands that day did not approve of the eruption of emotion he witnessed. He wrote, "Such frenzy as I saw there prepares the public systematically for hysteric

"MEND IT OR END IT"

emotions with all their consequences in social and political life."

The Harvard-Yale game wasn't the only game competing for America's attention that day. Douglas Carter, who played for Columbia University, took his position on the defensive line against the University of Pennsylvania. When he saw an opposing back come over the line of scrimmage, Carter lowered his head and plowed into him. The players running behind piled on too, adding their force to the already violent collision.

Carter suffered a "wrench of the spine" and was rushed to a hospital. The nurse was shocked at Carter's injuries. When she talked to Carter about the brutality of football, he defended the game saying, "It's not brutal, it's the greatest, the noblest, and the best game played."

Douglas Carter was one of the lucky ones that day.

New York University faced Union College in a game that was described as "very rough." Harold Moore, a nineteen-year-old halfback for Union College, got the ball on the 30-yard line and ran toward the goal. He was tackled and thrown down. Then a pile of players ended up on top of Moore.

HARVARD'S FOOTBALL CAPTAIN, DAN HURLEY, WAS UNABLE TO PLAY IN THE BIG GAME BECAUSE HE WAS IN THE HOSPITAL WITH A HEAD INJURY. CONSTRUCTION OF TEMPORARY SEATING ALLOWED FORTY-THREE THOUSAND FANS TO SQUEEZE INTO HARVARD STADIUM TO WATCH THE GAME BETWEEN HARVARD AND YALE ON NOVEMBER 25, 1905. THE TICKET PRICE WAS TWO DOLLARS EACH.

FOURTH DOWN AND INCHES

The referee blew his whistle because he feared someone would be hurt. A police officer ran onto the field to clear the pile of men. At the bottom of the stack, Moore was lying flat on his face. He was unconscious. Doctors in the crowd ran onto the field. One of them, Dr. Chester Whitney, announced that Moore was suffering a cerebral hemorrhage and was in very critical condition.

They couldn't wait for an ambulance, so someone brought around an automobile to take him to the hospital. Moore died at nine o'clock that night.

The *New York Times* declared, "His death was directly due, however, to concussion of the brain." A formal inquest was held to determine whether Harold Moore had been intentionally injured. After questioning witnesses, it was determined that Moore's death was an accident and that his fatal injury was the result of an impact with a single player.

| | | |

After the deadly 1905 football season, Nichols, the Harvard team doctor, wrote an article about the injuries of the year for the *Boston Medical and Surgical Journal*. According to Nichols, between September 12 and November 25, 1905, the Harvard football players

experienced a long list of injuries, including one brain hemorrhage; one broken cervical spine; five broken ribs; and a variety of broken fingers, wrists, noses, legs, cheekbones, pelvis, clavicles, etc.

And there were nineteen concussions. Nichols observed the following:

> The mental state of the players who had concussion was variable, some being highly excitable and hysterical, others merely confused, and in a few cases, knocked completely unconscious. In every case there was a certain loss of memory as to the facts occurring for a variable time subsequent to the injury. For instance, it was common to hear a player ask if he had played the first or second half of the game.

The doctor also commented on how the players viewed concussion. They saw it as a "trivial injury and rather regarded as a joke." Nichols consulted neurologists about the long-term effects of these concussions and reported that he "obtained very various opinions in regard to the possibility of serious after effects."

Nichols was way ahead of his time. More than one hundred years later, concussions would still be treated as trivial and regarded as a joke by some. It has only been in the last few years that medical science has come to a good understanding of concussions and their long-term effects on players.

By the end of the 1905 football season, nineteen men college age and younger died from playing football. Hundreds more suffered serious injuries.

One writer in the *New York Times* put it this way:

> If our colleges and universities were at war the record of nineteen killed in the course of a Fall campaign would not be deemed excessive. It would indeed be a rather moderate list of casualties. It is not bloody war, however, it is only football that brings together the students of these great institutions of learning.... When a game, a recreation, a pastime that boys engage in for their health results in the death of a considerable proportion of the contestants and in the more or less serious injury of many others it is evident that there is something the matter with the game.

| | | |

The three well-publicized football incidents—the injuries of Dan Hurley and Douglas Carter, and the death of Harold Moore—brought the battle over the brutality of football to a fevered pitch.

Universities had different views of the situation. Chancellor Henry MacCracken of New York University, the school whose team was playing against Moore's team, wanted to abolish football. The reasons for his decision were printed in the *New York Times*. First, "Its homicidal feature." Second, "The exaltation of bulk and brawn over brains." Third, "The exaltation of money making as a characteristic of the college game is, if possible, a worse evil." Chancellor James R. Day of Syracuse said, "One human life is too great a price to pay for all the games of the season."

On the other side, the former president of the Brown University Athletic Association said that if football was abolished, student life in American colleges would suffer. He believed the game developed "courage, co-operation, self-control, strength of purpose and generous enthusiasm."

The dangers and controversy of the game weren't just on the university level. The students of St. John's Academy, a high school in Manlius, New York, circulated a letter of protest against the way football was being played. They wrote, "[Football] is a great game gone to the bad. Let us resurrect its best features and save a noble sport. We want more game and less profession about it; more sport and less playing for blood; more open and less mass plays; more interference and less holding; more umpire and less slugging; more sprinting and less bucking; more brawn and less beef. Mend it or end it."

Columbia University decided to end it. Professor H. G. Lord, chairman of the committee that voted to abolish the game, said:

Only by such radical action can university and college life be rid of an obsession, which, it is believed, has become as hindersome to the great mass of students as it has proved itself harmful to academic standing, and dangerous to human life.

Coach Bill Morley, Columbia's football coach, did not agree with the committee's decision. The *New York Tribune* reported on December 2, 1905, the meeting between Columbia's president and the head coach. Coach Morely admitted football

THIS PHOTOGRAPH DEMONSTRATES THE ILLEGAL FOOTBALL MOVE OF A DEFENSIVE PLAYER STRIKING THE BALL CARRIER IN THE FACE WITH THE HEEL OF THE HAND. THIS WAS ONE OF THE MANY PRACTICES SPECIFICALLY PROHIBITED IN 1906.

had faults and that rules could eliminate some problems, but he did not want to do away with the element of danger entirely because, he said, "that is what draws the crowds."

Morley said, "The number of deaths from football this season was nineteen. The number last season was about the same." He defended the numbers by saying, "When you consider that during the football season probably 100,000 players are engaged in the game, the death rate is wonderfully small"—smaller than other sports, he argued. He firmly believed the rules of the game could be modified to "do away with some of the danger without detracting from the spectacular side of the sport."

Columbia's decision to end football caused a lot of controversy. Many Columbia students gathered in a huge meeting on December 4, 1905, to protest the abolition of football on their campus. Dr. H. Skelton Carter, the father of Douglas Carter, the injured player from Columbia, held with those who did not want to ban football. Although Dr. Carter said he didn't believe the game was "brutal or unduly dangerous," he added, "I will say, though, that having sons play the game detracts a great deal from the pleasures of it. I have had no enjoyment in watching the play, realizing there were dangerous possibilities in it, feeling a

natural anxiety of the safety of the players."

While few universities followed Columbia's lead to abolish football, most agreed the game needed to be changed from the way it was currently being played. Their actions launched a flurry of activity. According to the *New York Times* on November 30, 1905, Roosevelt did not think such radical action should be taken and believed "the evils of the sport can be eliminated and the game saved." As a next step, President Roosevelt called Reid back to Washington on December 4 to discuss the situation.

The Intercollegiate Rules Committee, with Walter Camp as chairman, also planned a meeting to discuss possible rule changes that would reform the game rather than abolish it. And New York University organized a meeting of colleges and universities on December 8, 1905, to discuss the following issues:

1. Should football be abandoned?
2. If not, what reforms are necessary to eliminate its objectionable features?
3. If so, what substitute would you suggest to take its place?

Strong opinions made for a stormy nine-hour meeting when sixty-two representatives from universities met to discuss what should be done about football. The meeting was full of "acrimony" and "bitterness." Eventually this large group agreed to choose a committee of seven men to work with Camp on rule changes.

Issues with football they believed should be corrected included: the need for a more open game (rather than mass plays like the flying wedge), the elimination of brutal play (such as kneeing, kicking, or slugging with a clenched fist), and the enforcement of the existing rules. Beyond these on-field issues, they agreed universities had to cease offering players money or support, professional athletes had to be barred from college teams, and recruiting preparatory school—high school—athletes must stop.

Camp's new seven-man committee that suggested the changes called itself the American Intercollegiate Football Rules Committee and later the Intercollegiate Athletic Association of the United States. In 1910 this committee would change its name again. It became the National Collegiate Athletic Association—the NCAA—which is today the main governing body for the multibillion-dollar college sports industry.

| | | | |

By the 1906 season, the committee had drafted new rules. Perhaps most notable to fans of the game today, the new rules allowed for "the forward pass"—where an offensive player throws to a teammate on the other side of the line of scrimmage—paving the way for modern football offenses. But the forward pass took years to catch on as a standard weapon. What really had immediate effect was the elimination of mass plays such as the infamous flying wedge.

Under the headline "The New Game of Football," the *New York Times* summed up the new rules:

> The main effort of the football reformers has been to "open up the game"—that is to provide for the natural elimination of the so-called mass plays and bring about a game in which speed and real skill shall supersede so far as possible mere brute strength and force of weight.

The rules would continue to evolve, but football's future was no longer under significant public threat.

| | | | |

Changing football rules didn't drastically reduce the number of football-related deaths. The

1909 season was even more dangerous than the 1905 season with the deaths of twenty-eight football players. Although the rules had technically eliminated mass plays, they were still happening. All but one of the players were killed as a result of a mass play. An article in the *New York Times* on November 28, 1909, described mass plays as these:

> Swift, startling blows, as it darts straight ahead through tackle or guard . . . piercing the line as if it were a knife going through a piece of cheese.

The article described the three-men-in-a-row mass formation that gathered momentum in a few strides as a "reaper in a field of grain." The article called for rule changes saying, "The ball is hidden in bewildering mass plays, unsatisfactory even to those spectators who understand what it is all about, and tremendously dangerous to the men engaged in them."

"IT WAS LIKE HAVING CHRISTMAS SIXTEEN TIMES A YEAR"

FOOTBALL DIDN'T JUST SURVIVE THESE TURBULENT YEARS; IT THRIVED AND BECAME FIRMLY ENTRENCHED IN AMERICAN CULTURE.

Football is on the minds of players, coaches, and fans long before the first hint of fall is in the air. Each year holds the promise of a winning season. On the first day of practice, no matter if he plays in the NFL, college, high school, middle school, or on a youth league team, each athlete walks onto the field as an individual. The players may have different opinions, beliefs, and ethnic backgrounds, but once they are on the gridiron, those differences melt away. On the field, they become one. This band of brothers become one team with one goal: win. And the same is true of the fans in the stands. Football is one of America's great unifiers.

The team bonds through the work, sweat, and pain of two-a-day practices, through the exhaustion and aching muscles, through the exhilaration of winning, and the disappointment of losing. Each teammate—from the starting quarterback to the benchwarmer—earns the right to wear his team's jersey. The team shares a sense of community, and each player values the contribution of all the other athletes. Each of the eleven men on the field is equally important. They work together as a team, each doing his assigned job.

Football not only unites teams, it also unites the school and the community. On Friday nights, stadium lights come on over high school fields all over America. In the brisk fall air, the team stretches in preparation for the battle ahead. The cheerleaders and drill team form the human tunnel their heroes will charge through. Batons twirl in the air. The band prepares for the halftime show. Popcorn is popping and hot dogs are warming in concession stands. The parking lot fills up, and fans make their way to the gate carrying blankets.

At last it is game time. The players put their hands over their hearts as the national anthem is played. The captains meet their opponent at midfield for the coin toss. The team is ready. They have been working for weeks for this moment. They are one.

The players never forget this moment.

| | | | |

Kevin Turner, a former NFL player, still remembers the excitement of his high school football days. He recalls, "When I woke up on game day, I couldn't wait until it was time for the kickoff. Wearing my jersey to school on game day was a big part of

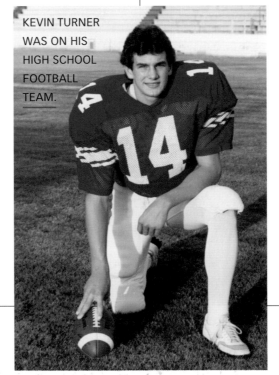

KEVIN TURNER WAS ON HIS HIGH SCHOOL FOOTBALL TEAM.

the experience. At game time, when I ran out on the field and heard the announcer call my name in the starting lineup, it was a rush like nothing else. It was like having Christmas sixteen times a year. My parents were proud of me. Nearly everyone in our small town was cheering in the stands and spontaneously reacting to what happened on the field. It was magical."

Today the glorious tradition of football stretches back more than a century. Millions of Americans today feel the same way about football as Douglas Carter did after his injury in 1905: "It's not brutal, it's the greatest, the noblest, and the best game played." Once the game starts, each athlete will give everything he has to win the game. No fear. No hesitation. No excuses. The coaches expect it. Teammates expect it. Each player expects it of himself.

Every fan in the stands can feel it when the players give it their all.

And if players "get their bells rung" or "get a ding" during the game, they shake it off. It is all part of the game.

Or is it?

FOURTH DOWN AND INCHES

"BELL RINGER"

FOOTBALL IS A "COLLISION SPORT," AND COLLISIONS HAVE BEEN ESSENTIAL TO THE GAME FROM THE BEGINNING. The result of a collision is often *trauma*—a term derived from the Greek word for wound. Both collisions and trauma are an accepted part of the game.

There are some football injuries that are easy to recognize like broken bones or torn tendons and ligaments. This type of injury was part of the game from its earliest days and an expected type of trauma that President Theodore Roosevelt did not "mind in the least." It was as much a part of the game then as it is now. Today when a player breaks a leg or blows out a knee, everyone sees and understands the injury. When he's carried off the field, the fallen hero is showered with admiring applause. The situation is clear and predictable.

But what about football injuries that are not easy to recognize like when a player gets a "ding" or a "bell ringer"? A player will sometimes keep playing, then manage to stumble off the field, unnoticed by coaches, cameras, or press. He might take a breather for a series or two. But he can walk, so he wants to play. He gets back in the game and back to his teammates. This too is as true today as it was one hundred years ago.

In football's early years, players thought of concussions as a "trivial injury and rather regarded as a joke." Player's attitudes didn't change much over the following century. And when Coach Reid of Harvard wrote in 1905 that he "placed more emphasis on his [player's] leg [injury] than I did on his head," he was among the first to minimize the seriousness of a player's head injury.

One major thing has changed in America's relationship with football, though. A century ago, when Nichols consulted neurologists about concussion, he wrote, "The real seriousness of the injury is not certain." Today the seriousness of concussions is certain. Medical experts understand that a football "ding" or a "bell ringer" is a concussion. Concussions are one of the most dangerous aspects of any sport. Especially football.

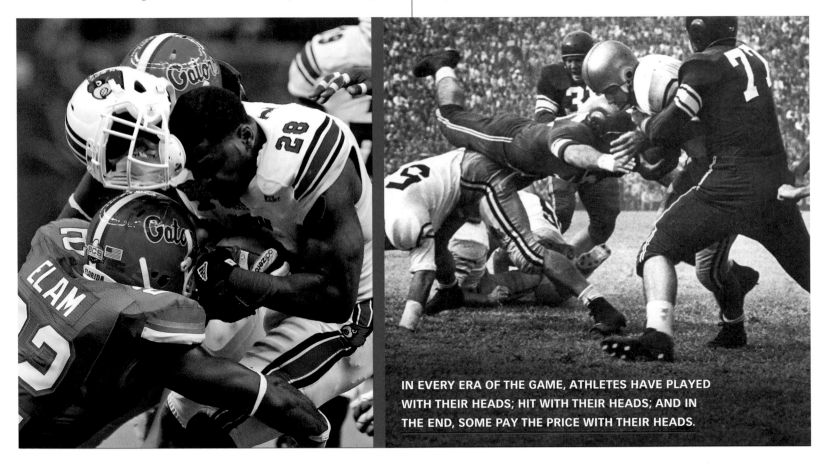

IN EVERY ERA OF THE GAME, ATHLETES HAVE PLAYED WITH THEIR HEADS; HIT WITH THEIR HEADS; AND IN THE END, SOME PAY THE PRICE WITH THEIR HEADS.

"TRAUMATIC BRAIN INJURY"

A COLLISION CAN WOUND BRAIN TISSUE AS TRAUMATICALLY AS IT CAN BONES, TENDONS, LIGAMENTS, AND MUSCLES. Scientists group many wounds to the brain under the heading traumatic brain injury, or TBI.

A TBI is an injury caused by an external force that disrupts the normal function of the brain. A traumatic brain injury could be the result of a bullet that pierces the skull and enters the brain or a hammer blow that depresses the skull against the brain. Or a TBI could be the result of a hit on a football field that jolts the brain back and forth inside an intact skull causing a concussion.

Concussions are not just a football or sports issue, of course. A concussion can be the result of falling on ice or a car wreck or any number of other accidents. They are a serious hazard for soldiers. But while a concussion can happen anytime, athletes are at higher risk.

Well over 8 million high school students play sports in the United States, and Dr. Dawn Comstock, a researcher at Ohio State University, has studied the number of concussions among that population. Although concussions happen in each of the twenty sports she studied, some sports have higher percentages of concussions than others. Using data from the 2008 to 2010 school years, the greatest numbers of concussions in high school sports come from football. The second-highest number of concussions happens in girls' soccer. The third-highest number comes from boys' wrestling.

Both girls and boys play some of the same sports like basketball and soccer, and Comstock's research also shows that in these sports, girls have a higher rate of concussion. The reason for this isn't clear. Some suggest it could be because of the physical differences in the head and neck. Others suggest girls are more honest about reporting their injuries than boys are.

▌ ▌ ▌ ▌

In recent years, medical science has gained a better understanding of the damage done by a TBI, how a concussion happens, and what a concussion really is.

A concussion is simply a TBI caused by a bump, a blow, or a jolt to the head that interferes with the normal function of the brain. Any type of brain injury is serious,

SKULL

BRAIN

CEREBROSPINAL FLUID

CEREBROSPINAL FLUID ACTS AS A LIQUID CUSHION, PREVENTING THE BRAIN FROM STRIKING THE HARD SKULL. THIS SYSTEM PROTECTS THE BRAIN FROM MOST SMALL BUMPS, BUT SOMETIMES IT ISN'T ENOUGH TO PREVENT THE BRAIN FROM CRASHING INTO THE SKULL.

especially when you consider that brain function controls so many bodily functions: movement, speech, hearing, memory, thought, personality, and so much else. The brain is also uniquely difficult to repair. A knee or a hip can be repaired or even replaced. And a person can live without an appendix, a gallbladder, or a spleen.

The brain cannot be replaced.

The human body protects this vital organ by surrounding it with the thick bone of the skull. Inside the skull, the brain is surrounded by cerebrospinal fluid, which keeps the soft, gelatinous brain away from the hard, rough bone inside the skull. The cerebrospinal fluid acts as a cushion to protect the brain during most of life's minor bumps and falls.

Even with this much protection, injuries happen. A bump, a blow, or a jolt to the head or the body can cause the brain inside the skull to stretch and move quickly. The brain can accelerate so fast—then stop so suddenly—that the cerebrospinal fluid cannot prevent the brain from slamming into the interior surface of the skull. The brain can bounce back and slam into the other side of the skull. These sudden movements can cause the cells in the brain to stretch and tear. These damaged cells cause chemical changes in the brain. This is a concussion.

A concussion does not mean the brain is bruised, bleeding, or swollen. A normal brain scan does not mean the patient did not suffer a concussion. In fact, no brain scan, blood test, or any other medical exam can diagnose a concussion. Because a concussion is an injury that interferes with the normal function of the brain, the only way to diagnose it is to identify a disturbance in the normal function of the brain. A medical professional diagnoses a concussion by carefully considering the symptoms reported by the injured person or the signs observed by others.

Recognizing a concussion after a head injury would be easier if *every* person experienced *every* symptom, *every* time. But that is not how a concussion works. In reality, when a person gets a concussion, he or she could experience one or more of at least twenty-six symptoms. Every

concussion is different, but each one is very serious.

One thing is certain though: unconsciousness is not a prerequisite for concussion. Studies show that only about 10 percent of people who experience a concussion lose consciousness.

Diagnosing concussion is always a problem, but it's a huge problem for football. And the consequences are equally huge. Consider two star quarterbacks of the mid-1980s NFL. On November 18, 1985, All-Star Washington Redskins quarterback Joe Theismann was hit by New York Giants linebacker Lawrence Taylor. The hit broke both of Theismann's lower leg bones and resulted in a compound fracture (a compound fracture is one where the bones come through the skin). The injury was so traumatic and gruesome that the *Washington Post* called it "The Hit That No One Who Saw It Can Ever Forget." There was no doubt Theismann had been seriously injured. Film of the play shows Taylor signaling frantically for help from the sidelines moments after the hit. And of course there was never any question that Theismann could continue to play and risk further damage to his leg. The severity of the injury was obvious. Joe Theismann never played football again after that game in 1985, and today, his right leg is shorter than his left.

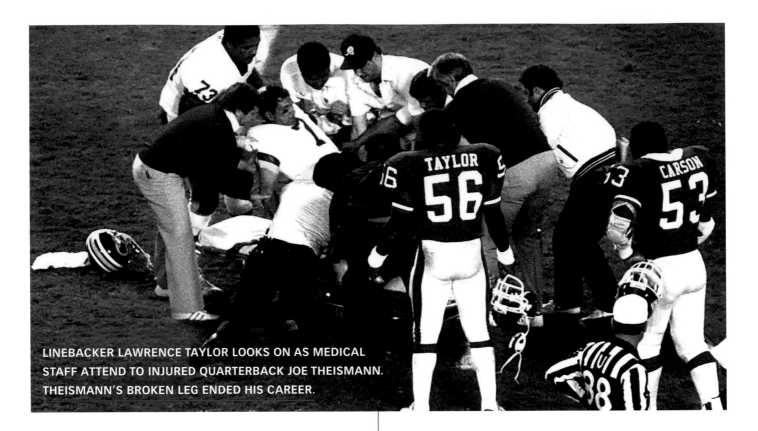

LINEBACKER LAWRENCE TAYLOR LOOKS ON AS MEDICAL STAFF ATTEND TO INJURED QUARTERBACK JOE THEISMANN. THEISMANN'S BROKEN LEG ENDED HIS CAREER.

That same year, quarterback Jim McMahon, who experienced several concussions during his fifteen-year career, led the Chicago Bears to victory in the Super Bowl. McMahon suffered one very public injury in the season following the Super Bowl victory when, after the play was over, Green Bay Packer player Charles Martin intentionally picked McMahon up and threw him down on his head and shoulder. Then a couple of years later, on October 12, 1988, the *Chicago Tribune* reported on an injury McMahon suffered in a game three days before. The trainer said, "He had a concussion, but it cleared by halftime. He lost his memory a little bit."

It is doubtful that an opposing player ever waved to the sidelines to help McMahon after a hit that caused his concussions. Like Theismann's, McMahon's injuries have affected him ever since. Today, McMahon often forgets why he walked into a room and gets lost in his own home. He was diagnosed with early-stage dementia at the age of fifty-three.

Two men with life-altering traumatic injuries. One was obvious even to someone watching on a tiny TV screen. One was completely invisible until it was too late.

FOURTH DOWN AND INCHES

"FOUR MILLION"

CONCUSSION HAS BEEN BIG NEWS IN FOOTBALL OVER THE LAST FEW YEARS, AND AWARENESS HAS SKYROCKETED SINCE JIM MCMAHON'S PLAYING DAYS. At the professional and college levels, games are huge televised events, and when a player's career or, worse, his life ends because of the effects of concussions, the event becomes a major story. And there have been many such stories.

It is rare for the topic of concussions in high school, middle school, and youth football players to rise to national prominence. Yet the number of professional and college football players combined is small when compared to the massive number of younger players.

There are approximately sixty-eight thousand college football players and seventeen hundred professional players. According to USA Football, a youth football partner of the National Football League, there are 1.14 million high school boys playing football and 3 million younger boys playing football in various youth leagues.

Professional and college football teams have doctors who treat injured players and athletic trainers who help them rehabilitate their injuries. At the same time, few of these four million boys playing football have this type of care. Most high schools and middle schools do not have an athletic trainer, much less a doctor nearby. In youth leagues, where young children even more susceptible to brain injury play, the coach is not usually a doctor or a trainer. Most likely, the coach is a father who volunteers because he loves the game. Often the coaches, parents, and players don't understand what a concussion is, how to recognize the symptoms and signs, or what should be done if a concussion is suspected. It isn't because they don't care—they care very much—it is because they don't know.

Although the numbers of reported concussions are on the rise, most experts believe the actual number of concussions is much higher than the number reported. Sometimes athletes won't tell anyone they are experiencing the symptoms of concussion because they don't want to appear weak or be taken out of the game or lose their spot on the team. Sometimes they don't even realize they are concussed.

| | | | |

When a bump, a blow, or a jolt causes the brain inside the skull to accelerate, it can move in two ways. If a person took a hit directly in the middle of his forehead—with or without a football helmet—with enough force, his brain would accelerate in a straight line and hit the back of the skull. Scientists call this a linear acceleration.

If a person took a hit that was slightly off the middle of his forehead or from the side with enough force (for example, a quarterback who gets "blindsided"), after the impact, his brain would rotate and hit the skull. This is called a rotational acceleration.

According to Dr. Robert Cantu, chief of neurosurgery at Emerson Hospital in Concord, Massachusetts, "On virtually every hit to the head, both the linear and rotational accelerations are present." Of these two types of forces, researchers believe rotational acceleration does more damage since blood vessels could stretch and tear as the brain rotates.

It may seem like a hard helmet-to-helmet hit would be the only type of hit that would cause a concussion, but that isn't the case. Players are at risk for a concussion during both practice and games as they collide with players, the ground, the goalpost, the bench, or other equipment. And a concussion can occur even without a direct blow to the head. If a jolt to the body causes the head to rapidly change speed in a sort of whiplash effect, the brain crashes into the skull in the same way it would if the blow was to the head.

While good equipment protects players from many injuries, it is not possible to completely

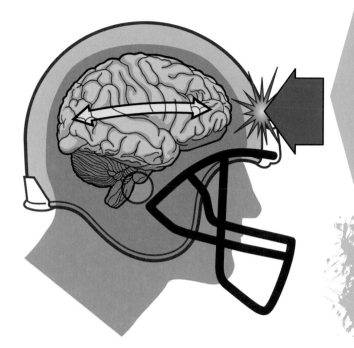

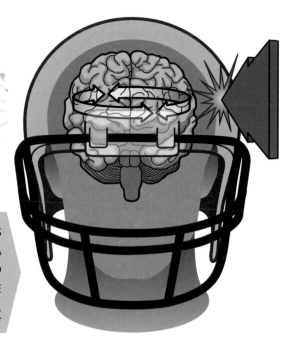

THE FIGURE ON THE LEFT SHOWS LINEAR ACCELERATION. A BLOW IN THE MIDDLE OF THE FOREHEAD COULD CAUSE THE BRAIN TO ACCELERATE IN A STRAIGHT LINE TOWARD THE BACK OF THE SKULL, THEN BOUNCE BACK TO THE FRONT.

THE FIGURE ON THE RIGHT SHOWS ROTATIONAL ACCELERATION. A BLOW FROM ANY ANGLE COULD CAUSE THE BRAIN TO ROTATE SLIGHTLY, THEN ROTATE BACK.

protect players from concussion no matter what sort of protective equipment they wear. During the earliest days of football, players did not wear helmets of any kind (eventually, some players used thin leather helmets to protect their ears). Later photos of football games show some players wore padded leather helmets and some didn't. As the years went by, hard plastic helmets replaced leather helmets. It wasn't until 1943 that the NFL required the use of helmets.

The purpose of football helmets is to prevent skull fractures. Football helmets do not prevent concussions today, and football helmets are very unlikely to prevent all concussions in the future.

The reason this is true becomes clear when you imagine what happens in the skull during a concussion. The brain accelerates, then suddenly stops, sending it slamming into the hard bones inside the skull. A helmet sitting on the outside of a player's skull cannot and does not prevent movement of the brain inside the player's skull. When a bottle of ketchup runs low, you shake it so the ketchup will come out faster. It isn't the acceleration of the bottle that moves the ketchup—it is the sudden stop. Now

DR. ROBERT CANTU IS ONE OF AMERICA'S LEADING AUTHORITIES ON SPORTS-RELATED CONCUSSIONS.

imagine that you placed the ketchup container in a helmet and shook it. When the helmet suddenly stopped, the ketchup would splat to the end even though it was "protected" by the plastic.

Or think of a bell. You ring a bell by moving it side to side, making the clapper inside strike the bell. Surrounding the bell in plastic and foam might make it ring less loudly, but it won't make the clapper hit the inside of the bell any less violently when you ring it.

The best and only protection from concussion today is knowledge. Players, coaches, athletic trainers, parents, and teachers must know what a concussion is, what causes a concussion, the symptoms and signs of a concussion, and what to do when a player is suspected of having a concussion.

FOURTH DOWN AND INCHES

"ARE WE IN PHILLY OR GREEN BAY?"

THE PLAYER LINES UP. HE CONCENTRATES ON HIS JOB. He anticipates his opponent's move. His blood is pumping. The ball is snapped. Instinct and memory of countless hours on the practice field take over. Like instruments in an orchestra blending together to play a symphony, every part of the player's body is working in perfect harmony.

In the player's brain, one hundred billion neurons are sending and receiving messages at lightning speed to make it all happen. Heart beats. Lungs breathe. Pick up your feet. Move your arm. Look at the coach. Remember the play. The neurons transmit these messages through a long fiber, called an axon, that is attached to each neuron. This information moves down the axon through an orderly chemical process. When the message gets to the end of the axon, a neurotransmitter transmits the message to the next cell. And so on. And so on.

Then *BAM!* An outside force causes the player's brain to crash into the side of the skull. Then the brain bounces off and crashes into the other side of the skull.

The brain, which had been busily transmitting countless messages, immediately reacts to this crisis. A chain reaction begins as chemicals in the brain move around in chaos. Message-carrying neurotransmitters are interrupted before they reach the axon. Suddenly, the brain can't send or receive messages normally.

Sometimes it happens as the result of a hard hit that everyone notices and leaves the player unconscious. Other times it happens as a result of a minor, routine play that no one but the player notices. The player could feel confused, have blurred vision, see stars, be off-balance, feel nauseous, or many other symptoms. Football players describe these symptoms as getting a "ding" or "getting their bell rung." To a neurologist, however, a traumatic brain injury has interfered with the normal function of the brain and caused a concussion.

Players often continue playing under these circumstances. Retired NFL player Kevin Turner recalls countless times throughout his football career when he "saw stars and had to blink my eyes, or shut my eyes and wait 15 to 30 seconds to get my balance back." He wouldn't say anything about it because the competitor in him wanted to go back on the field.

Players with a concussion have also been known to continue to play excellent football. Turner played even when he was so out of it that he had no recollection of the game later. He recalled, "I was with the Philadelphia Eagles in 1997. The game against Green Bay was in the Packer's stadium. On the opening kickoff, we set a wedge. I had my guy in my sights. That was the last thing I remember until the second quarter.

I was sitting on the sideline and looked around. I couldn't tell where I was. I asked one of my teammates, 'Are we in Philly or Green Bay?' He said 'Green Bay.' I asked 'How we doing?' I had played the whole first quarter and didn't know it."

Turner's buddy called the team doctor to take a look. The doctor had Turner follow his finger with his eyes and gave him a list of words to repeat. Finally, on the fourth try, Turner got all the words. After playing a whole quarter without knowing it, Turner missed only two series of downs. He returned to the game. He wanted to.

Toughness is part of the culture of football. T-shirts read: "Pain is weakness leaving the body," "Pain is temporary, pride is forever," "No pain, no gain."

One of the lessons learned from the game is to keep going no matter what. Players are sometimes asked, "Are you hurt, or are you injured?" The question means are you just hurting or are you really *injured*? A tough competitor doesn't want to complain about aches and pains because all the other guys have them too. They know what is expected: if you can walk, you can play. And there's glory in playing through the pain.

Consider another famous injury from the

1985 NFL season. San Francisco 49ers safety Ronnie Lott's fingertip was crushed during a game against the Cowboys. Today, the legend among players, fans, and even journalists is that Lott elected to have the tip of the finger amputated *during the game* so he could continue playing. Here's one writer in 2011 making an example of Lott while noting the rising concerns about concussion:

> Football is perceived as the ultimate man's game. Ronnie Lott, the 49ers' Hall of Fame safety, once had part of a finger cut off during the game so he could continue playing. And for decades playing through concussions was considered a sign of toughness, although now we are learning of just how silly and dangerous that line of thinking is.

THE LEGEND OF RONNIE LOTT'S AMPUTATED LEFT PINKIE IS OFTEN REPEATED AS AN EXAMPLE OF TRUE TOUGHNESS. THE REALITY WAS A LITTLE DIFFERENT.

Lott actually had the fingertip amputated in the off-season because it seemed simpler than having surgery to repair the finger. But the legend is more important than the reality, and the message couldn't be clearer: a real football player cares nothing for pain.

Yet even in the culture of toughness in football, some injuries are given necessary treatment and time to heal. When a player has an injury that causes a tear in the anterior cruciate ligament (ACL) of the knee—a very common football injury—he immediately stops playing and is sent for surgery and rehab. It often takes many months to rehabilitate a torn ACL. The player doesn't return to the field until he has fully recovered from the injury and is physically ready to compete. No

43

athlete will ignore symptoms of a possible ACL tear, yet many will ignore symptoms of a possible concussion. Retired pro Kevin Turner says, "I spent nine months rehabbing a knee and no time at all taking care of the most important part of me."

When a young player has a possible concussion, the coach or the athletic trainer should follow a clear concussion protocol. The player should not return to play for the rest of the game or practice. The player should be checked by a health-care provider who is experienced in evaluating concussions. And the player's parent or guardian should be informed and given information on concussions.

If the diagnosis is concussion, then the treatment is simple: rest.

In a way, this sort of rest is the brain's equivalent to keeping weight off a knee that has a torn ACL. If an athlete tore an ACL, he would rest it until it healed. He would not run a marathon on the injured leg. When he did walk, he'd use crutches. In a similar way, the brain needs to rest after a concussion. An injured brain needs both physical and mental rest while experiencing any concussion symptoms. Physical rest means no physical exertion and no risk of further head trauma. Mental rest means players should not stimulate

their brains—no texting, video games, TV, or computers. Since their brains need to rest from thinking and reasoning, school and schoolwork should be restricted. Allowing the brain to have time to rest from cognitive and physical activity gives the body time to repair itself. A brain injury is similar in this way to simply having a cut on the skin of your arm: in time, the body will heal the cut.

When a concussed player gives his brain rest and repair, 80 percent of all concussions are resolved in seven to ten days. Once a health-care professional determines the player is symptom-free for twenty-four hours, he can begin a gradual return to the game.

However, if he continues to play football without giving his brain time to rest and heal, he puts himself at great risk.

At minimum, playing football with a concussion may extend the length of time an athlete experiences symptoms, and research shows that concussion victims are more susceptible to future concussions.

More critically, playing football with a concussion puts players at risk of death from second impact syndrome (SIS). This occurs when a person who has not completely healed from a concussion, experiences a blow (often a minor blow) that sets into motion catastrophic brain damage. SIS disturbs how small blood vessels called arterioles control the blood flow into the brain. When SIS occurs, the arterioles dilate allowing a tsunami of blood to flood the brain causing the brain to swell. To illustrate the idea, think of a plastic water bottle placed in a freezer. As the water freezes, it expands, and the pressure causes the plastic bottle to bulge. When the brain swells and causes a dangerous amount of pressure inside the skull, death often occurs. People who survive SIS are usually left with severe disabilities.

In his research on second impact syndrome in high school and college players, Robert Cantu found ninety-four cases within a thirteen-year period. In his book *Concussions and Our Kids*, Cantu writes, "Almost all were high school athletes. Nearly three-quarters involved players who'd had a previous concussion that season. Approximately 40 percent were on the field despite having concussion symptoms at the time."

Although second impact syndrome is rare, it happens to football players every year.

"OVER EIGHT THOUSAND IMPACTS"

WHILE THE RISKS OF CONCUSSIONS IN FOOTBALL ARE MUCH BETTER KNOWN TODAY THAN THEY WERE EVEN A DECADE AGO, THERE IS STILL MUCH TO BE LEARNED ABOUT THE SCOPE AND MECHANICS OF HEAD TRAUMA IN THE GAME.

Football players today look as if they are well protected behind their pads and helmets—especially compared to photos of players a century ago. But what sort of blows to the head do the players really experience? Recent studies tell us. Dr. Steven Broglio, assistant professor of kinesiology and director of the Neurotrauma Research Laboratory at the University of Michigan, led a research team to study head impact of players on a high school football team in Illinois. The researchers reported their findings in the *Journal of Neurotrauma* in an article titled "Cumulative Head Impact Burden in High School Football."

They followed ninety-five high school football players over four seasons from 2007 through 2010. The researchers wanted to find out how many hits each player received—and how hard each hit was. To measure the hits, they used a Riddell Revolution helmet outfitted with a Head Impact Telemetry System (HITS) from Simbex.

HITS works by placing six accelerometers within the pads inside the helmet that record the location, magnitude, duration, and direction of head impacts. Information about head

THIS COMPUTER WIRELESSLY RECEIVES THE IMPACT DATA FROM THE ACCELEROMETERS INSIDE THE HELMETS.

AN INSIDE VIEW OF A RIDELL REVOLUTION HELMET FITTED WITH THE HEAD IMPACT TELEMETRY (HIT) SYSTEM. THE SIX ACCELEROMETERS PLACED IN THE PADS RECORD THE LOCATION, MAGNITUDE, DURATION, AND DIRECTION OF EVERY HEAD IMPACT DURING FOOTBALL PRACTICE AND GAMES.

impacts from each accelerometer is transmitted wirelessly to a computer on the sideline.

The players wore the helmets at every practice and every game throughout the entire season each of the four years. The data from each helmet was checked each day to ensure that any accidental impacts, like being dropped, were not included in the study.

During the four-year study, Broglio's research group followed the ninety-five players during 190 practices and fifty games. HITS measures impact in a unit of gravitational acceleration (symbolized g). Normal gravity on Earth causes objects to accelerate at a rate of 9.8 meters (32 feet) per second, for every second it falls—this is one g of acceleration. To put it into perspective, if you jumped up and then landed on your feet, you would experience about 10 g because you would have accelerated ten times that of gravity. During this four-year study, the researchers collected impact information on 101,994 hits from the ninety-five players.

The number of impacts and the severity of the impacts for each player were different depending on the position they played. The groups were broken down into five categories of players: linemen; quarterbacks; receivers, cornerbacks, and safeties; tight ends, running backs, and linebackers; and kickers.

The group's research found that quarterbacks received more impacts during a game than they did during practice. The other positions received more impacts during practice.

The researchers tracked the impacts in one season according to the playing position. Listed in the next column, you will see the player in these positions who received the least impacts and the players in these positions who received the most impacts. The number of impacts for the other players in these positions were somewhere in between.

LINEMEN

One of the linemen experienced seventy-three impacts in one season.

One of the linemen experienced 2,235 impacts in one season (a starting defensive tackle).

QUARTERBACKS

One of the quarterbacks experienced forty-nine impacts in one season.

One of the quarterbacks experienced 662 impacts in one season.

RECEIVERS, CORNERBACKS, AND SAFETIES

One player in these positions experienced forty-five impacts in one season.

One player in these positions experienced 895 impacts in one season.

TIGHT ENDS, RUNNING BACKS, AND LINEBACKERS

One player in these positions experienced seventy-four impacts in one season.

One player in these positions experienced 1,140 impacts in one season.

KICKER

The kicker experienced five impacts in one season.

The HITS accelerometers recorded the linear acceleration and the rotational acceleration of each impact. While the majority of impacts were in the 10 to 20 g category, the range of impacts received were anywhere from 10 g to more than 100 g. According to Broglio, an impact in the range of 90 to 100 g would be like ramming your head into a brick wall at 20 miles an hour. Over all the practices and games in one season, every position except kicker experienced at least one impact greater than 100 g at every practice and every game.

Considering his research and similar research on college football players, Broglio estimates that "a typical starting football player could therefore be expected to sustain over eight thousand impacts to the head during a combined four-year high school and four-year collegiate career."

I I I I

Another research group, Purdue Neurotrauma Group (PNG), a team at Purdue University including Dr. Larry J. Leverenz, Dr. Thomas M. Talavage, and Dr. Eric A. Nauman, designed a different sort of study. They knew some research was being done that followed college football players after they had been diagnosed with a concussion. Since little work of this type had

been done on the high school level, PNG wanted to study this group further. Their research would begin before a high school player suffered a concussion and then follow that player after the concussion.

The researchers included specialists in a variety of fields, including athletic training and therapy, brain imaging, the central nervous system, and musculoskeletal trauma.

The PNG team planned the study to include two parts.

First, they would use HITS accelerometers in the helmet of every player to record the location and intensity of every head collision at each full-contact football practice and game for the entire season. Second, they would measure the brain function of every player before, during, and after the football season. Following the athletes in this way would allow the PNG team to connect the players' brain function to the head trauma they experienced on the football field.

Next, they needed a nearby football team. Most of the football players, their parents, and the administration of nearby Jefferson High School in Lafayette, Indiana, allowed the PNG to gather research from the team. Before the first practice of the 2009 football season, each participating football player reported to the PNG researchers at Purdue University to begin.

For their research project, the researchers needed to know each player's usual brain function before the season began. In other words, they had to know the baseline for each player. With this information, researchers would be able to see if any injury decreased a player's ability to think. Also, if a player were injured and had a decrease in their ability to think, the baseline would allow them to know when the player's cognitive abilities returned to their "normal."

Before the first practice—and the first hit—of football season, the PNG researchers conducted two tests on each athlete. The first is a computer-based test called Immediate Post-Concussive Assessment and Cognitive Testing (ImPACT). This twenty-minute test measures how well the athlete remembers words and shapes as they go through a variety of sections. It measures the speed as well as the accuracy of their responses. The ImPACT test produces a score that represents their normal ability to think.

MEMBERS OF THE JEFFERSON HIGH SCHOOL FOOTBALL TEAM WERE MONITORED TO LEARN MORE ABOUT HOW IMPACTS AFFECT BRAIN FUNCTION.

The second test used functional Magnetic Resonance Imaging (fMRI), a type of medical imaging scanner that uses a powerful magnetic field to create an image. A fMRI scan shows how the brain is working. It can show how the brain handles functions such as thought, speech, movement and sensation. During the seven-minute fMRI, the athlete presses a button to respond to questions they are asked about pictures and symbols they see. The images of the fMRI show which parts of the brain were in use as the player responded.

At last, the players were ready for some football.

According to the HITS data, the number of hits each starting player took over the course of the season varied. One player received head hits 1,855 times during the season. The player with the lowest number of head hits was 226. Some of the hits were incredibly hard—at least one was 289 g.

During the ten-week season, the researchers repeated the ImPACT and fMRI tests on eleven players. These eleven players were in three

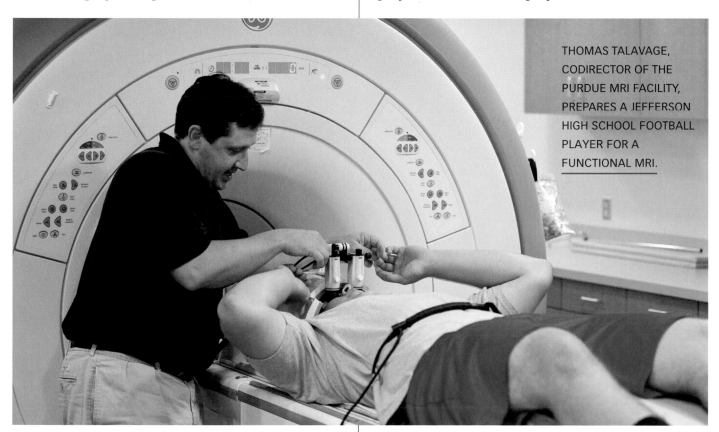

THOMAS TALAVAGE, CODIRECTOR OF THE PURDUE MRI FACILITY, PREPARES A JEFFFERSON HIGH SCHOOL FOOTBALL PLAYER FOR A FUNCTIONAL MRI.

"OVER EIGHT THOUSAND IMPACTS"

different categories. Three of the eleven had been diagnosed with a concussion. Four of the eleven had NOT been diagnosed with a concussion, and they received few head impacts. The remaining four of the eleven had NOT been diagnosed with a concussion, but they did experience a large number of head impacts and many hard hits (greater than 80 g).

After football season was over, the researchers repeated the ImPACT and fMRI tests on the same eleven players for the third time.

The researchers found what they expected to find in the first group. Because concussions interfere with the brain's normal function, the follow-up fMRI tests showed the brains of the three athletes who received a concussion diagnosis

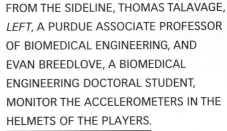

FROM THE SIDELINE, THOMAS TALAVAGE, *LEFT*, A PURDUE ASSOCIATE PROFESSOR OF BIOMEDICAL ENGINEERING, AND EVAN BREEDLOVE, A BIOMEDICAL ENGINEERING DOCTORAL STUDENT, MONITOR THE ACCELEROMETERS IN THE HELMETS OF THE PLAYERS.

were not working in the same way they did before the football season.

The PNG researchers expected no changes in the brain function of the eight players who did not have concussions, and as expected, the fMRI of the four players who had few head impacts showed no change.

When they looked at the results of the third group, the four players who had many head impacts but no diagnosed concussions, they were surprised. Nauman, an expert in brain trauma said, "At first we thought our scanner was broken. Then we realized this was a new group of impaired players." When the follow-up ImPACT test and the fMRIs of these four players were compared to their baseline tests, they each showed a change

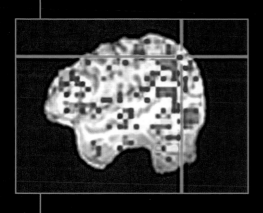
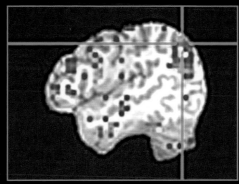

THIS PLAYER EXPERIENCED A CONCUSSION DURING FOOTBALL SEASON. THE fMRI SCAN ON THE LEFT IS THIS PLAYER'S BASELINE SCAN, WHICH SHOWS HIS NORMAL BRAIN FUNCTION. AFTER THE CONCUSSION, THE fMRI WAS REPEATED. THE SCAN ON THE RIGHT SHOWS A CHANGE IN HIS BRAIN FUNCTION.

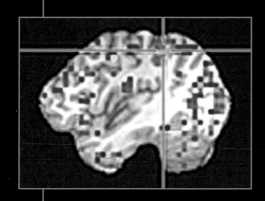
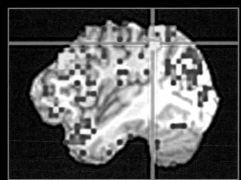

THIS PLAYER DID NOT EXPERIENCE A CONCUSSION DURING FOOTBALL SEASON. THE fMRI SCAN ON THE LEFT IS THIS PLAYER'S BASELINE SCAN, WHICH SHOWS HIS NORMAL BRAIN FUNCTION. THE FOLLOW-UP SCAN ON THE RIGHT SHOWS NO CHANGE IN HIS BRAIN FUNCTION.

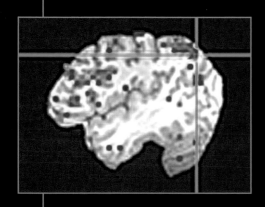
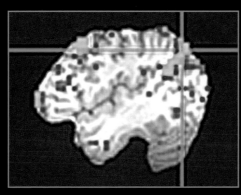

THIS PLAYER DID NOT EXPERIENCE A CONCUSSION DURING FOOTBALL SEASON. THE fMRI SCAN ON THE LEFT IS THIS PLAYER'S BASELINE SCAN, WHICH SHOWS HIS NORMAL BRAIN FUNCTION. THE FOLLOW-UP SCAN ON THE RIGHT SHOWS A CHANGE IN HIS BRAIN FUNCTION. THIS GROUP OF PLAYERS CAME AS A SURPRISE.

in brain function. The part of their brains that were not functioning as before was the area that is associated with working memory, which lies just above the forehead. And on almost every play, these players had impacts just above their foreheads.

The scientists looked at the data collected from the helmet accelerometers for these four players. The players, mostly linemen, received many helmet-to-helmet hits. Nauman said, "These are the kids who put their head down and take blow after blow to the top of the head. We've seen this primarily in linebackers and linemen, who tend to take most of the hits."

The PNG researchers were stunned. They did not expect to find any neurological changes in any of the football players that had not experienced a concussion. But the proof was right in front of them.

These four players did not have concussions; they did not have any symptoms of concussion. But the brains of these four players were not working the way they did before football season. All four showed impaired brain function. And their brains showed just as many neurological changes as the players who were diagnosed with a concussion.

This was new information.

The PNG research indicates that some players do not have any symptoms or signs of a concussion, yet their brains are not functioning as before. Talavage, an expert in brain imaging, sums it up this way: "They're not exhibiting any outward sign and they're continuing to play. The cognitive impairment that we observed with them is actually worse than the one observed with the concussed players."

These changes in their brain function, although unknown and unseen, may make athletes vulnerable to a concussion. This may explain why some players get a concussion after a minor hit rather than a huge, hard tackle.

"To be taken out of a game you have to show symptoms of neurological deficits—unsteady balance, blurred vision, ringing in the ears, headaches, and slurred speech. Unlike the diagnosed concussions, however, these injuries don't affect how you talk, whether you can walk a straight line, or whether you know what day it is," said Leverenz, an expert in athletic training and therapy.

The risks are clear. "If you have traumatic brain injury and keep playing, you are at enormous risk of really serious damage later on. Because these kids don't show any symptoms, they keep playing and exposing themselves to neurological trauma," said Nauman.

Leverenz explained, "The problem is that the usual clinical signs of a head injury are not present. There is no sign or symptom that would indicate a need to pull these players out of a practice or game, so they just keep getting hit."

The research done by the PNG indicates disturbing aspects of repetitive head injuries from football. The study indicates some football players who have not sustained a concussion and do not have any symptoms of concussion still have damage. And that damage is equal to the players who had been diagnosed with concussion.

This research also suggests that a concussion from football may not be the result of one blow but an accumulation of blows.

In some cases, a player might sustain a life-altering injury *without showing any outward signs*. The implications of these finding are potentially game changing.

| | | | |

The human brain is not fully developed until about the age of twenty-five. Repetitive brain trauma on still-developing brains puts young people at risk. These recent research studies on high school football players indicate some of the problems that can result from concussive and sub-concussive blows to the head.

While teens are at risk, younger players are even more vulnerable to head injuries. Until about fourteen years old, children's heads are large in comparison to their bodies. The muscles in their necks are weak, which means when they experience an impact, they can't brace for a hit like an adult can. According to Cantu, a child's brain takes longer to recover from a concussion than an adult's brain. He is also concerned that children who begin playing tackle football this young may experience so much total brain trauma that it may put them at risk for long-term health problems.

When people see a team of young boys dressed in a full-pad football uniforms, they may think the boys couldn't possibly tackle one another with much force. However, a research project completed by the Center for Injury Biomechanics at Virginia Tech may challenge this way of thinking. The researchers published their findings in an article titled "Head Impact Exposure in Youth Football" in the *Annals of Biomedical Engineering*.

As with similar studies on high school players, the research team would use accelerometers inside the helmets to measure the number and severity of impacts. Seven players aged seven to eight wore the special helmets during every practice and every game.

Over the football season, each of the seven players received an average of 107 hits. The majority of the hits (59 percent) occurred during practice. None of these seven players were diagnosed with a concussion.

The surprising part of this study was the force of hits experienced by seven- and eight-year-old children. The helmet accelerometers measured impacts that ranged between 10 and 100 g. One impact during the season reached 100 g. This means that in one hit, a little boy experienced the same force he would have felt if he ran headfirst into a brick wall at 20 miles an hour. During the season, six impacts over 80 g were recorded. The force of these impacts is of the same severity as those experienced by high school and college football players.

As was the case a century ago, stakeholders in football have met the concern about injury with rule changes. Pop Warner Little Scholars is a youth football league for children, five to fifteen. Pop Warner has been around for almost a century, and each year about 250,000 children participate in Pop Warner football. Beginning in the 2012 season, Pop Warner rules stipulate that there be "no full speed head-on blocking or tackling drills where players line up more than 3 yards apart" and that "the amount of contact at each practice will be reduced to a maximum of 1/3 of practice time."

Is this enough to make football safe for children under fifteen? Until more scientific studies are completed, it isn't possible to say. But the long-term risks are staggering.

"THE BRAIN BANK"

"CUCKOO! CUCKOO! CUCKOO."

The fans screamed toward the boxer in the ring as he stumbled like he was intoxicated. In the 1920s, a prizefighter like this was said to be "punch drunk."

Dr. Harrison Martland described this condition, known by its medical term *dementia pugilistica,* in 1928 in the *Journal of American Medical Association* in an article titled "Punch Drunk." The condition was caused by too many blows to the head. He described the condition as one that began with unsteadiness, slight mental confusion, and slow muscle action. It progressed to "hesitancy of speech, tremors of the hands, and nodding movements of the head." The boxers ended up with mental deterioration, and some were put in asylums. Martland said that about half of the fighters who stayed in the sport long enough ended up with this condition.

Today the condition has a different name: chronic traumatic encephalopathy (CTE). The name simply means a long-term disease caused by brain trauma. It was believed for many years that CTE was found exclusively in boxers.

That is, until Mike Webster.

"Iron Mike" Webster played 245 games in his seventeen years as a professional football player, mostly for the Pittsburgh Steelers. Webster had four Super Bowl rings and was inducted into the Hall of Fame. He was known as a tough competitor and a hard worker on the field.

But the last years of Mike Webster's life were troubled ones. He showed signs of dementia, a deterioration of intellectual functions. He was homeless for a time. He struggled with drug use. He was in such physical pain that to get relief, he would shoot himself with a Taser to knock himself out.

"Iron Mike" Webster died on September 24, 2002. News reports said Webster died after a heart attack. He was fifty years old.

Dr. Bennet Omalu saw Webster for the first time at Omalu's workplace—the Allegheny County Coroner's Office. Omalu is a neuropathologist—a scientist who studies diseases of the brain and nervous system. It was Omalu's job to conduct an autopsy on the famous Steeler lineman.

When Omalu examined Webster's brain, he found CTE. Until that point, this disease had only been seen in the brains of boxers. Yet,

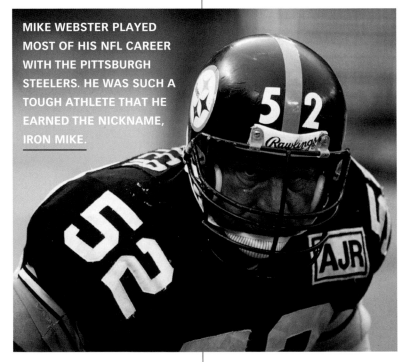

MIKE WEBSTER PLAYED MOST OF HIS NFL CAREER WITH THE PITTSBURGH STEELERS. HE WAS SUCH A TOUGH ATHLETE THAT HE EARNED THE NICKNAME, IRON MIKE.

there was no doubt. Webster had CTE.

It was the first time CTE had been connected to a football player. It wouldn't be the last.

The same year Webster died, Christopher Nowinski began his career as a professional wrestler. Nowinski was not your usual wrestler type. He had played four years on the football team at Harvard University. In 2000 he graduated with honors from Harvard after earning a degree in sociology.

Nowinski's persona and wrestling name became Chris Harvard. As Chris Harvard, he wore crimson shorts with a big H for Harvard on the seat. In the ring, he bragged about his superior intelligence—and insulted the lack of intelligence of his challenger. The Ivy League snob arrogantly trash-talked his opponents with chants like, "Five, ten, fifteen bucks, we'll own the companies, you'll drive the trucks."

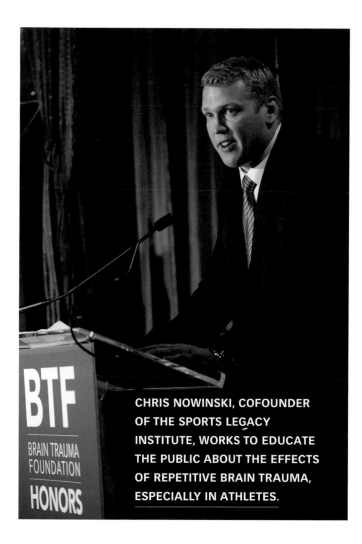

CHRIS NOWINSKI, COFOUNDER OF THE SPORTS LEGACY INSTITUTE, WORKS TO EDUCATE THE PUBLIC ABOUT THE EFFECTS OF REPETITIVE BRAIN TRAUMA, ESPECIALLY IN ATHLETES.

During a wrestling match in 2003, his opponent's boot crashed into Nowinski's chin causing a concussion. In his book, *Head Games*, Nowinski described how he felt: "Something was wrong with my vision. I didn't know where I was, what was happening around me, or why I was staring up at fuzzy-looking lights on the distant ceiling of a gigantic arena—I only knew that something was terribly wrong. I looked to the side, and saw thousands of people staring back at me. I gazed up at Nick [the referee]. I didn't want to move. My head felt like it was in a vise."

Nowinski didn't know that blow would change the course of his life.

Days passed after that blow, but Nowinski still felt rotten. He went back into the wrestling ring, but his symptoms continued. During matches he couldn't remember the sequence of events that were supposed to happen next. He had trouble focusing. His head pounded when he worked out. Headaches continued and got so bad he couldn't laugh or read or concentrate. He couldn't remember the names of people he knew. He couldn't sleep. He was depressed.

Nowinski finally made an appointment with Cantu. In addition to being chief of neurosurgery at Emerson Hospital in Concord, Massachusetts, Cantu is the leading sport concussion expert in

He was good at what he did, and crowds loved to hate bad guy Harvard. He was named youngest male Hardcore Champion in WWE and named Newcomer of the Year by *Raw Magazine*.

the country. In 1986 he wrote the first return-to-play guidelines for athletes with concussion.

When Cantu asked Nowinski how many concussions he had ever had, Nowinski answered with a range of zero to one. Cantu explained that a concussion is actually a problem with brain function and showed Nowinski the list of concussion symptoms. He asked him if he had ever experienced any of those symptoms after getting hit. Nowinski looked at the symptoms and remembered his past injuries. He realized he had experienced at least six concussions.

Cantu told Nowinski that his slow recovery could be because he'd had repeated concussions. Like many patients who come to see Cantu, Nowinski was suffering from post-concussive syndrome, a condition when intense concussion symptoms last an unusually long time. Some people have symptoms such as headaches, problems concentrating, poor memory, and sleep problems that can last for weeks, months, and even years in some cases.

Research indicates that once a person experiences one concussion, they are more likely to have more. And oftentimes, later concussions occur as a result of less force than the first one. Also, the more concussions a person experiences, the longer it takes their brain to recover.

Nowinski continued to suffer with post-concussive syndrome. He wanted to learn more about concussions and began reading research on the topic. He realized there was a concussion crisis in the making. Nowinski decided to do something about it.

In 2007 Nowinski and Cantu cofounded an organization named the Sports Legacy Institute (SLI). The mission of the institute is to advance the study, treatment, and prevention of the effects of brain trauma in athletes and other at-risk groups.

The next year, the Sports Legacy Institute partnered with the Boston School of Medicine to form the Center for the Study of Traumatic Encephalopathy (CSTE). Dr. Ann McKee, a neurologist and a neuropathologist, joined them as a codirector of the CSTE. She is a professor of neurology and pathology at Boston University School of Medicine and directs the Neuropathology Service for the New England Veterans Administration Medical Centers. McKee began the "brain bank" at the Bedford Veterans Administration Medical Center in Massachusetts to study Alzheimer's disease. When the CSTE was created, McKee oversaw the creation of a different brain bank devoted to the

DR. ANN MCKEE, CODIRECTOR OF THE CENTER FOR THE STUDY OF TRAUMATIC ENCEPHALOPATHY (CSTE), OVERSEES THE BRAIN BANK AND STUDIES THE BRAINS THAT ARE DONATED TO THE CSTE. MCKEE IS A NEUROLOGIST, A NEUROPATHOLOGIST, AND A FOOTBALL FAN.

study of the brains of athletes and veterans who had experienced head injuries. It is now the world's largest brain bank for athletes.

A donated brain can't save a life directly in the way a donated liver or kidney might. But a donated brain may help save countless lives in the future by helping researchers better

understand brain trauma.

The brain bank at the CSTE is crucial to the ongoing research on the long-term effects of concussions on athletes. At this time, CTE cannot be diagnosed in a living person. To diagnose CTE, researchers like McKee must study the brain after death. Each brain donated

"THE BRAIN BANK"

to the bank allows McKee to learn more as she continues her work.

| | | |

CTE is a disease found only in the brains of people who have experienced repetitive brain trauma. The sort of repetitive brain trauma that causes CTE is the result of thousands of blows to the head—like those experienced by athletes over their lifetimes in many different sports including boxing, hockey, soccer, and football. While it is likely that some of the thousands of blows an athlete receives throughout his or her career will cause a concussion, the majority of blows will not result in a diagnosed concussion. These are considered subconcussive blows—hits that could be damaging but do not cause any symptoms.

Scientists know something about how CTE works in the brain. Repetitive hits to the head causes tau, a protein in the body, to build up in the brain. This buildup of tau appears as neurofibrillary tangles (NFTs). NFTs in a distinctive pattern in the brain prove the presence of CTE.

Research shows that once CTE begins in the brain, it is progressive. In other words, CTE doesn't stop even if the activity that caused it (like football) stops. Once CTE starts, the damaged areas get bigger and the damage becomes more severe. As a result, the symptoms continue to worsen. The cells that are damaged can no longer transmit messages through the brain as they should. When enough cells are damaged by CTE, the brain doesn't work properly. Then symptoms become noticeable.

| | | |

Virginia Grimsley knew something was wrong with her husband, John, a retired linebacker who played for nine seasons in the NFL. John Grimsley began having memory problems. He'd even forgotten about his son's engagement party that he'd help plan. Unfortunately, this was not the worst lapse.

On February 6, 2008, John Grimsley was cleaning a gun, as he had done many times before. Only this time the gun was still loaded. He accidentally shot himself and died from his injuries. After his death, Virginia Grimsley wondered if his memory problems had anything to do with the nine concussions he experienced during his football days. She decided to donate her husband's brain to the CSTE brain bank.

When McKee studied the brain of John Grimsley, she found evidence of CTE. He was forty-five years old.

TO LOOK FOR EVIDENCE OF CTE, LABORATORY STAIN IS APPLIED TO THE BRAIN SAMPLES. NORMAL BRAIN TISSUE DOES NOT ABSORB THE STAIN. DAMAGED BRAIN TISSUE DOES ABSORB THE STAIN, WHICH SHOWS UP AS BROWN PATCHES.

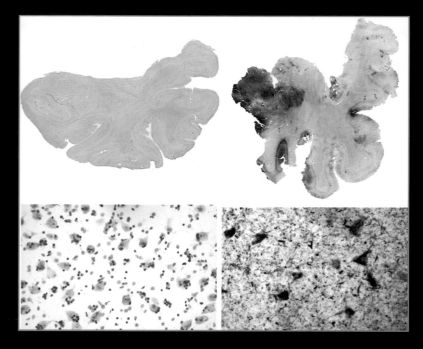

LEFT TOP: A SLICE OF A NORMAL BRAIN FROM A SIXTY-FIVE-YEAR-OLD DONOR, NOT DAMAGED BY CTE.

LEFT BOTTOM: A MAGNIFIED VIEW OF A NORMAL BRAIN NOT DAMAGED BY CTE.

TOP RIGHT: A SLICE OF BRAIN FROM RETIRED NFL PLAYER JOHN GRIMSLEY. THE BROWN AREAS SHOW DEPOSITS OF TAU PROTEIN THAT PROVE THE PRESENCE OF CTE.

BOTTOM RIGHT: A MAGNIFIED VIEW OF JOHN GRIMSLEY'S BRAIN, WITH EVIDENCE OF CTE.

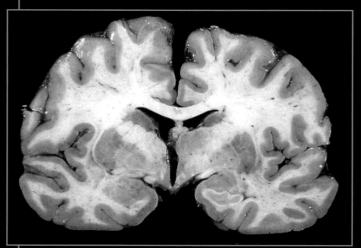

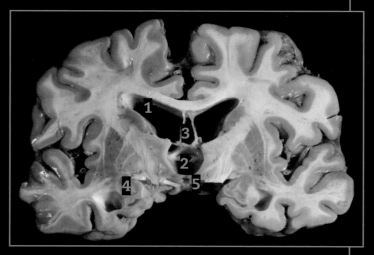

THE BRAIN SAMPLE ON THE LEFT IS NORMAL—NOT AFFECTED BY CTE. THE BRAIN SAMPLE ON THE RIGHT COMES FROM A RETIRED PROFESSIONAL FOOTBALL PLAYER WHO HAD CTE. IN LATE STAGES OF CTE, CHANGES IN THE BRAIN CAN BE SEEN WITHOUT MAGNIFICATION. AREAS 1, 2, AND 3 ARE DILATED, OR BIGGER THAN THEY SHOULD BE. AREAS 4 AND 5 ARE ATROPHIED, OR SMALLER THAN THEY SHOULD BE.

63

"OUR MINDS ARE WHO WE ARE"

TOM MCHALE WAS THE GUY EVERYBODY WISHED THEY COULD BE. He made everyone he met feel special. He loved life. And he loved football. The only thing he loved more than football was his wife, Lisa, and their three sons. McHale knew he was fortunate to have lived his dream of playing as an offensive lineman in the NFL for the Buccaneers, Eagles, and Dolphins. After nine seasons, McHale retired. He knew his body just couldn't take one more season.

After he hung up his pads for the last time, McHale enjoyed running his successful restaurants. Even though his football days were in the past, the constant pain in his shoulder was a daily reminder of the physical game he'd played

for many years. It had become part of his life, and he never complained about it to his wife.

Slowly, Lisa began to see a change in her husband. He became irritable and depressed. He no longer followed his morning routine of getting up at five to exercise and read his Bible before breakfast. He didn't enjoy any of the things he used to, such as music, cooking, or his restaurants. She soon found out that her husband was addicted to prescription pain medication.

McHale got help with his addiction, and his wife looked forward to the return of the man she loved, the one who had been her best friend since college. But even after McHale was off drugs, he was different. He was restless,

On the evening of May 25, 2008, McHale told a friend he was going to get help with his problem. A few hours later, the forty-five-year-old died in his sleep, with drugs in his system.

Lisa McHale donated her husband's brain to the Center for the Study of Traumatic Encephalopathy. Since her husband had never been diagnosed with a concussion, she was sure he did not have CTE. But she thought his brain could be helpful as part of their research as an example of a professional player's brain without damage from concussions.

discontent, and confused. He had trouble remembering things. He made lists of things he needed to do but didn't do any of them. McHale wrote in his diary that he "was overwhelmed by the continual feeling that he was having a nervous breakdown."

He relapsed back to his addiction of prescription drugs and started taking illegal drugs too. McHale tried again and again to stop his drug addiction. No matter how hard he tried, the once disciplined, goal-oriented athlete could not get control of himself.

She was stunned when she learned the truth. Tom McHale had CTE. McKee explained that the part of his brain that commands judgment and impulse control was heavily damaged. According to McKee, in the life of a person who had this sort of damage, "you would expect the symptoms of lack of insight, poor judgment, decreased concentration and attention, inability

TOM AND LISA MCHALE WITH THEIR THREE SONS, CHRISTMAS 2003

to multitask and memory problems."

Lisa McHale looked at the slides of her husband's damaged brain tissue. She was overcome with sadness as she realized CTE was likely the cause of many of his problems, including his drug addiction. She understood that his confusion was beyond what he could control. She said, "He was losing his mind. And our minds are who we are."

She made the connection between CTE and football—the only facet on his where he'd experienced head trauma. She says, "I lost my very best friend and my kids lost their dad. It seems a heavy price for playing a game."

It seems Tom McHale was one of many retired professional football players who battle depression. In 2007 Dr. Kevin Guskeiwicz gathered information from 2,552 retired pro players and published "Recurrent Concussion and Risk of Depression in Retired Professional Football Players" in *Medicine & Science in Sports & Exercise*. This study made the connection between concussions and depression. His research revealed that players who received three or more concussions during their football careers were three times more likely to experience clinical depression than retired pro players who did not receive a concussion.

"I COULDN'T PUT A NUMBER ON THAT"

KEVIN TURNER SAW THE BALL SPINNING THROUGH THE AIR. Years of practice, instinct, and natural talent kicked in as he reached for it.

It was his rookie year in the NFL after being the third-round draft pick of the New England Patriots. His team was playing against the Cleveland Browns in front of thousands of screaming fans.

Turner caught the ball on the 15-yard line. He tucked the ball in the crook of his arm and ran as he'd never run before. He didn't slow down until he crossed into the end zone.

"Oh my God, I scored a touchdown in the NFL!" he thought.

This was the moment he'd dreamed of all his life. It was happening. It was real. Tears welled up in his eyes and ran down the cheeks of the 6 feet 1 inch, 230-pound fearless athlete. And he couldn't stop them. Sweat and tears poured down Turner's face as his teammates patted his shoulder pads and congratulated him.

He sat down on the bench and put his head in his hands. Nothing else mattered at that moment as he took in the realization of his childhood dream.

"Turner. Turner. Turner."

He was touched that his teammates were so happy for him that they were calling out to him. Of all people, these guys understood what this moment meant to him.

Then it hit him. They were calling his name

because he was supposed to be on the field for the kickoff. He ran onto the field to do his job. At the start of the next play, the tears were still coming.

It was an experience Turner will never forget.

Kevin Turner has always loved football. He started playing tackle football when he was five years old, continued through youth football, junior high, and high school. He was a talented player who helped his high school team win the state championship in his home state of Alabama. He attended the University of Alabama and was cocaptain of the Crimson Tide team where he was the starting fullback in forty-one consecutive games. He played eight seasons in the NFL.

Turner isn't sure how many concussions he's had. During his career, players were only considered to have a concussion if they were

KEVIN TURNER AT THE AGE OF TEN. HE'D BEEN PLAYING FOOTBALL FOR FIVE YEARS WHEN THIS PICTURE WAS TAKEN.

unconscious. Turner had been knocked out twice. But when he thinks back over the many times he saw stars, had blurred vision, had ringing in his ears, or experienced other symptoms of concussion, he says, "I couldn't put a number on that." He kept playing no matter what. He explains, "At the time, as soon as you knew your name and where you were, you're ready to go back in and play."

"If I felt a little woozy or got a little blurry-eyed sometimes, I really wouldn't say anything about it. That's the way I was. If I wasn't knocked out, I probably didn't say anything. The competitor in me wanted to go back out there. They wanted me out there."

Turner's football dream ended when he retired at the age of thirty-one. But the effects of the pounding his body took through the years stayed with him. He battled depression, headaches, memory loss, and addiction to pain medication. Ultimately, he went bankrupt and got divorced—all things he never dreamed he would experience.

A few years ago, Turner picked up his guitar. But for some reason his fingers wouldn't reach the G chord he was looking for. Doctors tried various treatments, including neck surgery, to solve the problem, but something was still wrong. His left arm felt weak. Then his right arm did too.

In May of 2010, he finally got the diagnosis. He has amyotrophic lateral sclerosis (ALS), commonly known as Lou Gehrig's disease. ALS is a fatal disease that affects the nerve cells in the brain and spinal cord. As the disease progresses, the deteriorating neurons no longer send messages to the muscles. Slowly, patients lose the ability to move their limbs. When the muscles in the

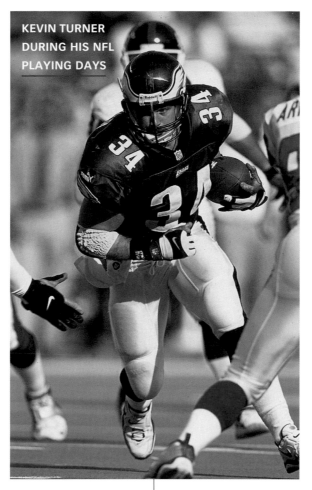

KEVIN TURNER DURING HIS NFL PLAYING DAYS

diaphragm and chest wall stop working, patients are unable to breathe.

Turner believes his ALS is connected to his football career. And new research seems to support that belief. Everett J. Lehman and his research team studied the cause of death of 3,439 NFL players who had played for at least five seasons between 1959 and 1988. The researchers' purpose was to find out how many deaths were caused by the neurodegenerative conditions of Parkinson's disease, Alzheimer's disease, and ALS. Their findings were published in *Neurology* under the title, "Neurodegenerative Causes of Death among Retired National Football League Players."

The researchers found that the incidence of Alzheimer's disease and ALS was four times higher in retired NFL players than in the general U.S. population. Also, the researchers

"I COULDN'T PUT A NUMBER ON THAT"

found higher rates of Alzheimer's disease and ALS in the players who played speed positions (quarterback, running back, halfback, fullback, wide receiver, tight end, cornerback, safety, and linebacker).

▌ ▌ ▌ ▌

As medical research reveals connections between repetitive head injuries in football to neurological problems, rule changes have been made at all levels of the game. Perhaps more changes will be made in the future. And now as a century ago, it's not hard to find fans who do not want any changes to be made to the game they love. But fans experience the game while sitting in the stands or on the couch. Players experience the game through bone-rattling hits.

Turner says, "There are big time collisions. Let's not take a step back to the Roman era where we're putting football players up there with gladiators. It's a game. It's entertainment. It's a dream of theirs, like it was of mine, but it's not worth their living that last 20 years of their lives with dementia, Alzheimer's, or ALS."

Turner still loves football. He knew playing football in the NFL came with a risk. He accepted that after he retired, he might be left with aches, pains, arthritis, and a bad back. But he never imagined he'd be diagnosed with ALS

at forty-one years of age. Turner says, "When I was playing in the NFL, I would have never imagined a day where I couldn't button my own shirt or zip up my pants."

ALS has taken a lot away from Turner, but not his sense of humor. With his easy southern charm he jokes, "The first doctor said she thought I had twelve to fifteen years [to live] then I saw another doctor that said five or six. The third doctor said you have two or three years. Heck, I'm going to stop going to see doctors. I may not make it out alive next time."

Turner has chosen to use his situation to make a difference in the world. He founded the Kevin Turner Foundation to bring attention to the disease and to financially support efforts to study, treat, prevent, and ultimately cure ALS. He also wants to raise awareness about brain trauma in athletes and bring attention to the possible connection to ALS. "I see this disease as an opportunity, and the Kevin Turner Foundation is an opportunity. You know everybody eventually has to die. I am just blessed to be reminded of it each day so I can make every moment count."

Turner has already committed to donating his brain to the CSTE after his death. He knows they will find evidence of ALS. He also expects them to find CTE.

"THE THING ABOUT FOOTBALL"

NATHAN STILES WAS A WILD CHILD. ACTIVE. FEARLESS. DETERMINED. He did everything at full speed. He didn't slow down for anything, even though it meant he got more than a few bumps, bruises, and gashes along the way. Growing up, his parents taught him to channel that energy into doing his best in whatever he did. Nathan did just that. By the time he was in his teens, he was a straight-A student, a good singer, active in his church, and a natural leader at Spring Hill High School in Spring Hill, Kansas. He had a quirky side too: he liked to eat Cheerios in water instead of milk.

At nearly 6 feet tall and 175 pounds, Nathan was a good athlete. Even though he was a humble guy, his good looks, easy smile, and the mischievous twinkle in his hazel eyes earned him the nickname of Hollywood. In his small town of five thousand people, Nathan was the sort of boy every mama hoped her daughter would date.

Going into his senior year, Nathan looked forward to his favorite sport, basketball. But first came football season. Nathan had played football since seventh grade—or at least he played when he wasn't injured. He'd had some football injuries that kept him out of play for periods of time, including a broken collarbone his sophomore year. Nathan had no plans to play college football. He didn't even want to play in his senior year of high school but decided to go ahead and finish his football career with the rest of his team.

As a senior and natural leader, Nathan was chosen to be a captain. Like everything else he did, he took this responsibility seriously. He gave football 100 percent. In early September, he broke his left hand playing football. It took surgery, a metal plate, and six screws to fix the broken bones. He never complained, even though his injury kept him out of the next two games. He still went to practice every day. When his teammates ran plays, Nathan ran laps. By the fourth game of the season, Nathan wrapped up his hand and played anyway. He started at running back and linebacker. Like generations of football players before him—all the way back to the earliest days—Nathan played through the pain for the sake of his team, and he didn't complain.

The fifth game for the Broncos was October 1—homecoming at Spring Hill High. During

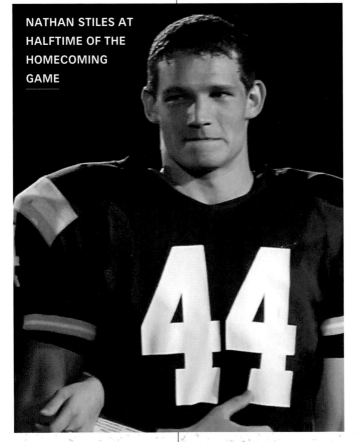

NATHAN STILES AT HALFTIME OF THE HOMECOMING GAME

the halftime festivities, Nathan was surprised to be named Homecoming King. Honored but a bit uncomfortable with the attention, he stepped forward to receive his crown. He was still wearing his purple and gold uniform. Soon the royalty marched off the field. Nathan took off his crown and put his helmet back on for the second half of the game.

Although no one knows when, at some point during the game, Nathan sustained a concussion. Nathan played the Homecoming game as usual, but his team lost 17–0.

When Nathan got up the next morning, he told his mom, "I have a headache."

"How did you get a headache?" she asked.

"Oh, I think I just got knocked around a little yesterday," he said.

On the following Tuesday while doing drills at practice, Nathan told his coach, "My head keeps hurting, and every time I make contact I've got a headache."

He was immediately pulled from practice. The next day, Connie Stiles, Nathan's mom, took him to the emergency room. CT scans of Nathan's brain were normal. Following the concussion protocol, his doctor kept him out of football until he was symptom-free, then waited longer still before beginning the return-to-play protocol.

Even though Nathan's mom didn't want him to return to the field, he wanted to play again.

NATHAN, CHOSEN AS HOMECOMING KING AT SPRING HILL HIGH SCHOOL, IS SHOWN WITH THE HOMECOMING QUEEN.

After all, he only had two games left.

His first game back was October 22, senior night. As usual, Nathan's parents watched him play. Once as Nathan walked back to the huddle, his mom thought he seemed a bit stunned, but nothing extraordinary happened during the rest of the game.

Even though his team lost, Nathan was pleased with how he'd played. After the game, Nathan told his dad, "I've never felt better. That was the best game; I've never felt so good." The next day he took the ACT test.

A few days later, Nathan came home from practice and looked inside the refrigerator for his usual treat. His mom watched as Nathan grabbed his jar of applesauce, took off the lid, and chugged some down.

"I'm glad tomorrow is the last football game. I'm ready for basketball and a change of pace," Nathan said.

"You always say that, even at the end of basketball season," his mom teased.

"Yeah, but the thing about football is it can kill you. With basketball, you just lose a game," Nathan answered.

The next day, on October 28, was the last game of the season. Nathan didn't plan to play football in college, so he knew it would be the last competitive football game he would ever play. The first half was amazing. Nathan played the best game of his life, rushing for 165 yards and scoring two touchdowns. When Nathan ran with the ball, he moved with a graceful flow that his father, Ron, described as "just beautiful."

But during Nathan's longest touchdown run that night, he seemed to stumble a bit about 20

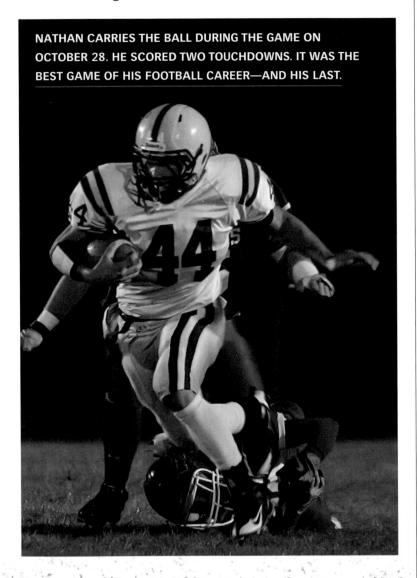

NATHAN CARRIES THE BALL DURING THE GAME ON OCTOBER 28. HE SCORED TWO TOUCHDOWNS. IT WAS THE BEST GAME OF HIS FOOTBALL CAREER—AND HIS LAST.

yards from the goal line. His dad remembers thinking something didn't look right. Then a few plays later, Nathan missed a tackle. Ron Stiles said, "It just didn't seem like him."

On a routine play about two minutes before halftime, Nathan came off the field to the sideline. His mom watched him from the visitors' bleachers on the other side of the field. She knew the way her son walked, and something didn't seem right. He disappeared behind the line of players standing on the sideline.

As Nathan neared his buddy on the sideline, he grabbed his head and screamed, "My head, my head."

His friend knew something was wrong, badly wrong. He used his cell phone to call Nathan's family in the bleachers. Nathan collapsed. The friend called the Stiles family again and told Nathan's mom to come to the field immediately.

Connie Stiles raced to the sideline. When she saw Nathan, he was on the ground in front of the bench. Unconscious. She talked to Nathan, trying to get him to respond. Nothing. She kept talking. His left arm lifted, then fell. He had a seizure.

Then nothing.

Soon a helicopter ambulance arrived. Nathan's parents, sister, and grandmother watched as he was loaded in, and with a blur of the blades, the helicopter took off. His family ran to their car for the hour's drive to join him at the hospital.

Back at the field, the two football teams and officials met at midfield and took a knee. One of the coaches on the opposing team said a prayer even as Nathan was on the way to the hospital.

At the hospital, the doctors told Nathan's family that his brain was bleeding. To stop it, they must operate.

The waiting rooms filled with friends. Then the halls filled with friends.

Surgery stopped the bleeding. But Nathan's brain was damaged. There was nothing more the doctors could do. Nathan's lungs filled with fluid. His heart began to fail. Only hours before, Nathan ran across the goal line for a touchdown. Now he lay in the intensive care unit. Nothing could stop what was happening.

Ron and Connie Stiles knew. They decided to share Nathan with those who loved him and waited in the halls. In groups of three or four, Nathan's friends came to his side to say good-bye.

Nathan died at four in the morning on October 29, 2010, nearly 113 years to the day after Von Gammon died in Georgia in one of the first football tragedies.

| | | |

Nowinski from the Center for the Study of Traumatic Encephalopathy made the call. He's made many similar calls, but it never gets any easier. He asked Nathan's parents to consider

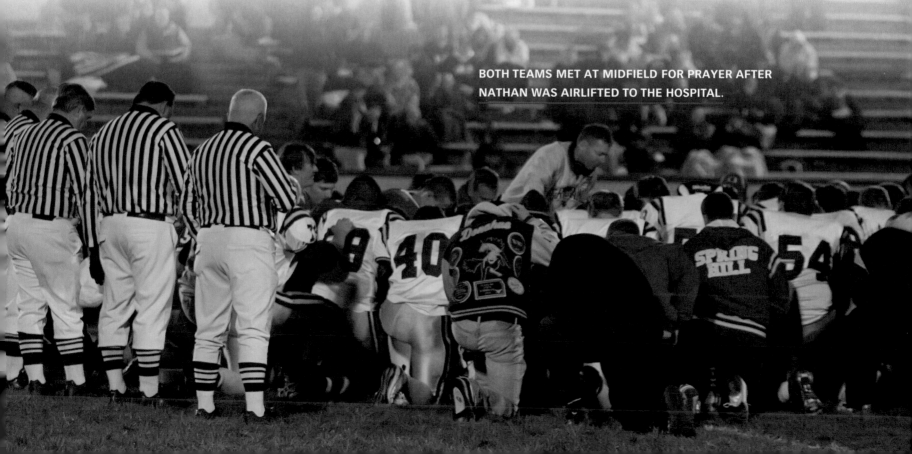

BOTH TEAMS MET AT MIDFIELD FOR PRAYER AFTER NATHAN WAS AIRLIFTED TO THE HOSPITAL.

donating Nathan's brain to the brain bank to help researchers study the connections between football, concussions, and CTE.

Nathan's father recalled a conversation he'd had with his son. Nathan saw the organ donation information on the back of his father's driver's license and asked his dad what it meant. His dad said, "It means that you would allow your organs to be donated to people who need them, if something happened to you."

"I'm OK with that, I wouldn't need them anymore." Nathan said.

Nathan's parents agreed to donate Nathan's brain to the CSTE. They also donated his other organs to be used for transplantation.

No one was prepared for what came next. McKee found CTE in Nathan's brain. It surprised McKee to see it in a seventeen-year-old. She said, "You expect a pristine brain. I saw a brain that was riddled with tau proteins. I was stunned at how similar that brain was to the boxers who lived into their 70s."

Nathan is the youngest person found to have CTE. There is only one cause for a person to develop CTE: repetitive brain trauma. Nathan's parents asked Cantu to review his case. His opinion is that Nathan's first injury caused a subdural hematoma—a collection of blood on the surface of the brain—that hadn't completely healed. On the night Nathan died, the injured area began to bleed again. A CT scan of Nathan's brain indicated that in addition to this, he may also have experienced second impact syndrome.

Following the death of Von Gammon more than a century ago, banning football in Georgia was a possibility. Von's mother defended the game her son loved, describing it as the "most cherished object of his life." After Nathan's death, there was no talk of banning the game. But if there had been, his mother would not defend football the same way. Perhaps because football was not the most cherished object in Nathan's life—to him it was just a game. Connie Stiles believes risk is part of everything in life, including football. She also believes you can't live life in fear. She hopes players, coaches, and parents will become better informed about the danger of concussions.

Ron and Connie Stiles do not blame anyone for Nathan's death—not football, not the coaches, not the opposing teams, and not the doctors. Instead of focusing on the details of what caused Nathan's death, they choose to focus on the meaning of his life. They created the Nathan Project, a ministry that gives away Bibles—which was the most cherished object in Nathan's life.

"SEVENTEEN PERCENT"

CTE HAS BEEN FOUND IN THE BRAINS OF PEOPLE WHO HAVE BEEN DIAGNOSED WITH CONCUSSIONS. CTE has been found in the brains of people who have *not* been diagnosed with concussions. CTE has only been found in people who have experienced repetitive head injuries. CTE has *never* been found in the brain of a person who does not have a history of repetitive head injuries.

Medical experts believe the risk factor for developing CTE is the total brain trauma—which is concussive blows that cause symptoms and the thousands of sub-concussive blows that don't cause symptoms. It doesn't make any difference how the brain trauma occurs. It could happen while playing football, boxing, wrestling, hockey, soccer, skiing, banging your head against a wall, or some other way. Cantu says "You cannot condition the brain to taking blows. If you subject the brain to enough head trauma, permanent brain damage may happen."

Yet, not everyone who has a history of repetitive brain trauma will develop CTE. For people who have experienced concussions or repetitive head injuries, it is impossible to know what effects—if any—they may have in the future. It is impossible to know who will develop CTE and who will not. At least as of today, there is no answer to explain why some athletes develop the disease and others do not, just like there is no answer to explain why one person who smokes cigarettes gets lung cancer and another does not.

Some retired NFL players show no signs of any problems and enjoy successful careers in the public eye. Joe Theismann—the Redskin's quarterback whose shattered leg ended his career in 1985—appeared on TV to comment on NFL games for two decades after his injury. He continues to work in football broadcasting today. Theismann is not alone. Many other former NFL players have been spared devastating long-term problems. Yet Jim McMahon struggles with dementia. "Iron Mike" Webster's life took a dramatic turn for the worse almost immediately after his retirement. They're not alone either. Other retired NFL players who during their lives battled depression, addiction, impaired judgment, and deteriorating mental capacity were diagnosed after death with CTE. Some committed suicide. As of this writing, about four thousand former players and families have joined together to sue the NFL claiming the league concealed the dangers of concussions.

In 2009 McKee wrote, "Most sport-related head injury is minor and although the majority of athletes who suffer a concussion recover within a few days or weeks, a small number of individuals develop long-lasting or progressive symptoms. This is especially true in cases of repetitive concussion or mild traumatic brain injury in which at least 17 percent of individuals develop chronic traumatic encephalopathy (CTE)." Since McKee wrote these words, her research has continued. Now, McKee believes the percentage of people with a history of repetitive head injury that will develop CTE is higher than 17 percent.

Today, much is known about repetitive brain trauma and CTE—like the fact that once CTE develops it slowly progresses and cannot be stopped. But much more needs to be learned. Researchers hope to find a way to diagnose CTE while the athlete is still alive. Then they hope to find a treatment. Ultimately they want to find a cure and prevent CTE from happening in the first place. Families who donate the brains of their loved ones for study allow McKee and other researchers to advance knowledge of this disease. The Center for the Study of Traumatic Encephalopathy has a bank of 135 brains; 80 percent of them show signs of CTE. More than six hundred athletes have pledged their brains after their deaths to advance this research.

Where does football go from here? Is it possible once again to make football safer?

Slowly some changes are happening. In 2011 the NFL agreed to reduce the number of full-contact practices to fourteen a season. The Ivy League passed new rules to limit the number of full-contact practices to two a week (and the NCAA permits five). And Pop Warner teams will limit contact in practice.

Cantu writes, "The philosophy I preach to my patients is as follows: No head trauma is good head trauma. If knocking around the brain can be avoided, then avoid it." He believes kids younger than fourteen should not play tackle football, and the number of hits during high school football during practice should be reduced.

To reduce the number of times a young athlete is exposed to repetitive brain trauma, the Sports Legacy Institute developed a program for athletes under eighteen called Hit Count. The program suggests no child would receive "more than 1,000 hits to the head exceeding 10g's of force in a season, and no more than 2,000 times in a year."

Hit count is similar to the pitch count used in Little League baseball. Pitch counting seeks to protect young athletes from elbow and shoulder injuries by limiting the number of pitches and requiring rest between pitching sessions. If a pitch count is necessary to prevent injury to an arm, it should be even more critical to prevent injury to the brain. After all, a person can live without an arm, but not without a brain.

It is true that keeping track of the number of hits to the head of a football player is not as simple as counting pitches. Hit count would require technology to track the hits, and that takes money. Cantu says, "If we don't take action, we will live in the safest country in the world for a young boy to have an elbow, and the most dangerous country for him to have a brain."

It is only in the past few years that doctors and researchers have begun to better understand the connection between football, concussions, repetitive brain injuries, and CTE. It takes time for the results of medical research to reach the general population. For example, it took years before the connection was understood and accepted that there is a link between smoking and cancer, drinking during pregnancy and fetal alcohol syndrome, or a high-fat diet and heart disease.

The dangers of repetitive head injuries and CTE have been known in the world of prizefighting for many years. While watching a boxing match, it is easy for a spectator to understand that getting punched in the head over and over again can't be a good thing for a brain. But for some people, it is harder to accept that the same thing is happening on the football field.

In players who do develop CTE, years pass between the time repetitive head injuries occur and the first sign of a problem. Meanwhile, each year millions of football players continue to play even though they often don't know what a concussion really is or recognize the symptoms and signs of a concussion or understand the serious health risks of playing with a concussion.

It isn't only the players who don't understand. Many coaches, trainers, and parents don't understand the dangers of concussions or repetitive head injuries. Since research in this area is relatively new, some medical doctors are not up to date on the latest treatment recommendations unless they have had continuing education in this area. This is why experts recommend that a concussed athlete should see a health-care professional who is experienced in evaluating concussions.

The results of a survey of high school football players in *ESPN The Magazine* reveals that a better understanding of the long-term risks is needed. The survey asked, "Is having a good chance of playing in the NFL worth the possibility of permanent brain damage?" One player answered, "Yes, you can make enough money to live with brain damage." Another said, "I would sacrifice the long-term possibilities for that opportunity to play in the NFL. Hopefully by the time I get older, there might be better medicine and care for former players in the NFL."

The survey also asked, "If your team was playing for the state title and your star player suffered a concussion, would you rather lose the game because the star player was out of the game, or would you rather win the game because he risked playing with a concussion?" One player answered, "Win the game. That would be a once-in-a-lifetime opportunity. Wounds heal, memories last forever."

Unfortunately, in some cases, he's wrong on both counts.

| | | |

Every football player comes to the end of his career. For some it is in high school, for others in college. A fortunate few live their dream of playing in the NFL. No matter how important the play, the game, or the season, sooner or later the game is over. The cheers stop. The stadium lights are turned off. The crowd goes home. The achievements of most players are forgotten as fans look forward to next season.

After the last game of a player's career is over, a lot of life is ahead of him. As the years go by, he won't want to forget the sights, sounds, smells, and excitement of playing the game he still loves.

He will need a healthy brain to remember them.

"EVERYTHING I HAVE"

A NOTE FROM THE AUTHOR

My personal experiences are one of the reasons I wanted to write this book. Yet, when I began the research, I didn't fully realize how close to my life this topic would come. My youngest son, Corey Andrew Killough McClafferty, died from a head injury. He was not a football player. He was fourteen months old. Corey experienced two minor falls—but they occurred within twenty-four hours of each other. While researching this book, I came to understand as I didn't before that my son's first fall caused a concussion. That concussion had not had time to heal before the second fall, which resulted in second impact syndrome.

Corey's life—and his death—is always with me. Because of this, what you read in these pages about concussions and traumatic brain injury is more than "head" knowledge from a writer, it is also "heart" knowledge from a mother.

One of the athletes I discovered in my research epitomizes how deeply athletes love their sports.

Eric Pelly was a superb athlete who loved football and played it for much of his young life. In his junior year of high school, he chose to play rugby rather than football. By his senior year he moved up to a semipro rugby team. Though he wasn't on the field, he was at every football game as the team's biggest and loudest fan.

During a rugby game on September 30, 2006,

he suffered a concussion when an opposing player's knee slammed into Eric's temple just as his head hit the ground. After sitting a while on the bench, Eric fell to the ground clutching his head in pain. He was rushed to the hospital where scans were normal. He was told to stay away from contact sports for three months and that he could work out when he felt up to it.

Even though he had a headache, Eric went back to his usual activities and schoolwork. On October 10, ten days after his last concussion, Eric and his family were gathered around the kitchen table for dinner. He was talking to his little sister when suddenly Eric's eyes rolled back in his head. He had a seizure and fell out of his chair, unconscious. His father performed CPR until the ambulance arrived. Medical professionals tried to resuscitate him at the hospital, but Eric was gone.

ERIC PELLY'S FOOTBALL PHOTO DURING HIS SOPHOMORE YEAR IN HIGH SCHOOL

After his death, his family found out that Eric had experienced a concussion they knew nothing about. It had happened at a rugby match on September 16—only two weeks before his last game.

The Pellys donated their son's brain to the CSTE. Once again, the results came as a surprise. Eric's brain showed evidence of CTE.

Eric wasn't one to write poetry, yet for a class assignment a few days before his death and while he was likely still suffering headaches from his concussions, he handed in a poem that was about a subject near and dear to his heart. I've chosen that poem for the epigraph of this book because I think it's important that the very first—and now last words—come from someone who loved sports. We must remember how deep the passion for a game often runs. This is not now and will not ever be a simple issue.

PLAYING SPORTS

is my life…

I Live….

Eat….

Breathe…

and Dream

of the

Action….

the Excitement….

the Competition.

The wild

adventure of

each new GAME is

like walking on the

edge of

the HORIZON,

knowing

whatever is at the

END I will have

given to the game

EVERYTHING
I HAVE!

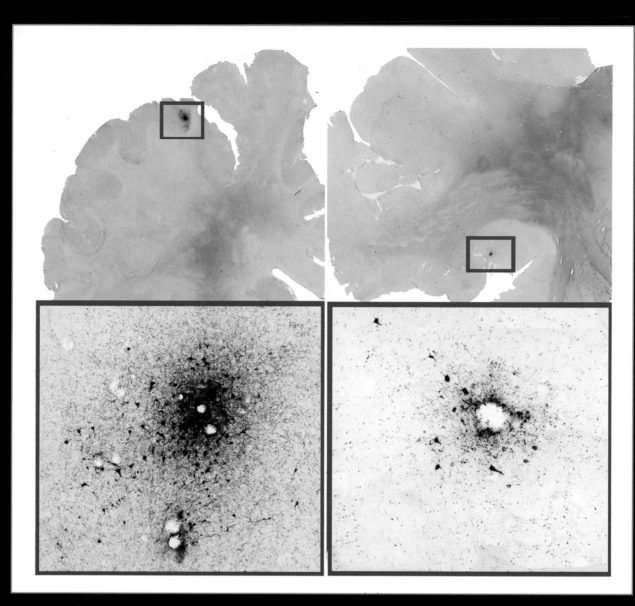

ERIC PELLY'S BRAIN TISSUE SHOWS EVIDENCE OF CTE. THE BROWN AREAS INDICATE
A BUILDUP OF TAU PROTEIN, WHICH ABSORBED THE LABORATORY STAIN. THE BOTTOM
IMAGES ARE MAGNIFICATIONS OF THE TOP IMAGES.

CONCUSSION SYMPTOMS

According to Dr. Robert Cantu, chief of neurosurgery at Emerson Hospital in Concord, Massachusetts, the symptoms of a concussion fall into four different categories:

PHYSICAL (SOMATIC)

Headache or head pressure

Nausea and/or vomiting

Balance problems

Vision problems such as blurred vision

Dizziness

Don't feel right (got a "ding" or "your bell rung")

Sensitivity to light

Sensitivity to noise

Loss of consciousness

Fatigue or low energy

Neck pain

Numbness and tingling

Ringing in the ears

THINKING/REMEMBERING (COGNITIVE)

Confusion

Difficulty thinking clearly or concentrating

Difficulty remembering

Feeling slowed down

Feeling in a fog

EMOTIONAL

Irritability

Feeling more emotional

Sadness

Nervousness, anxiety

SLEEP DISTURBANCE

Drowsy

Sleeping more than usual

Trouble falling asleep

Sleeping less than usual

RETURN TO PLAY

The Center for Disease Control (CDC) Heads Up program provides the following Return to Play Progression for athletes who have experienced a concussion. Each step in the Return to Play Progression takes a minimum of one day. For more information, see www.cdc.gov/concussion/headsup/return_to_play.html.

BASELINE

As the baseline step of the Return to Play Progression, the athlete needs to have completed physical and cognitive rest and not be experiencing concussion symptoms for a minimum of twenty-four hours. Keep in mind, the younger the athlete, the more conservative the treatment.

STEP 1: LIGHT AEROBIC EXERCISE

The goal: only to increase an athlete's heart rate

The time: five to ten minutes.

The activities: exercise bike, walking, or light jogging

Absolutely no weight lifting, jumping, or hard running

STEP 2: MODERATE EXERCISE

The goal: limited body and head movement

The time: reduced from typical routine

The activities: moderate jogging, brief running, moderate-intensity stationary biking, and moderate-intensity weight lifting

STEP 3: NONCONTACT EXERCISE

The goal: more intense but noncontact

The time: close to typical routine

The activities: running, high-intensity stationary biking, the player's regular weight-lifting routine, and noncontact sport-specific drills. This stage may add some cognitive component to practice in addition to the aerobic and movement components introduced in steps 1 and 2.

STEP 4: PRACTICE

The goal: reintegrate in full-contact practice

STEP 5: PLAY

The goal: return to competition

6 Joan Pelly, personal communication with the author, March 6, 2013.

8 George Magruder Battey Jr., "Anecdotes and Reminscences." *A History of Rome and Floyd County* (Atlanta: The Webb and Vary Company, 1922. 343–348), available online at http://books .google.com/books/about/A_History _of_Rome_and_Floyd_County _Statentml?id=xvbTT88nRmoC (November 19, 2012).

10 *New York Times*, "Football Rules Near to Ideal," March 4, 1917.

10–11 Ibid.

11–12 *New York Times*, "No More Football for Cadets," October 25, 1894.

12 *New York Times*, "No Scoring in the Second," November 25, 1894.

12 Ibid.

14–15 *St. John Daily*, "Football Attacked by Eliot," February 6, 1906.

15 *New York Times*, "Football Conference Called for Next Week," November 30, 1905.

15–16 *New York Times*, "Abolish Football Says Harvard Bulletin," October 19, 1905.

16 *New York Times*, "A Defense of Football," November 16, 1905.

16 Theodore Roosevelt, *Presidential Addresses and State Papers: May 10, 1905 to April 12, 1906,* Volume 4. (Whitefish, MT: Kessinger Publishing, 2006).

17 Ibid.

17 Ibid.

17 *New York Times*, "Reforming Football to Reduce Injuries," October 15, 1905.

17 Ibid.

17 *New York Tribune*, "Believes In the Game," 21 Nov. 1905.

18 Ibid.

18 Bill Reid and Ronald A. Smith, *Big-Time Football at Harvard, 1905: The Diary of Coach Bill Reid* (Urbana: University of Illinois Press, 1994), 194–195.

19 Ibid., 206.

19 Ibid.

19 Ibid.

19 Ibid., 207.

20 *Pittsburgh Press*, "Captains Have Been Chosen," December 4, 1904.

20 Reid and Smith, 297.

20 Ibid.

20 Ibid., 301.

21 Ibid., 304.

21 Ibid., 306.

21 Ibid., 306–307.

21 Ibid., 308.

21 *New York Times*, "Hurley Badly Injured," November 24, 1905.

21 Ibid.

21 Ibid.

21–22 *New York Tribune*, "Football Not Target." December 2, 1905.

22 *New York Times*, "Carter Fast Recovering," December 2, 1905.

22 Ibid.

22 *New York Times*, "Football Player Killed." November 26, 1905.

23 Ibid.

23 *Harvard Current*, "Physical Side of Football," January 5, 1906.

23 Ibid.

23 Ibid.

24 *New York Times*, "The Homicidal Pastime," November 29, 1905.

24 *New York Times*, "Abolition of Football or Immediate Reforms," November 28, 1905.

24 *New York Tribune*, "Football Not Target."

24 Ibid.

25 *New York Times*, "Football Is Abolished by Columbia Committee," November 29, 1905.

25 Ibid.

26 *New York Tribune*, "Football Not Target."

26 *New York Times*, "Football Is Abolished by Columbia Committee."

26 *New York Times*, "Carter Fast Recovering."

26 *New York Times*, "Football Conference Called for Next Week."

26 *New York Times*, "Football Conference Will Convene Today," November 30, 1905.

27 *New York Times*, "Football Convention Wants One Rule Code," December 29, 1905.

27 *New York Times*, "The New Game of Football," September 30, 1906.

27 Ibid.

28 *New York Times*, "Football Sport in Jeopardy," November 28, 1909.

28 Ibid.

28 Ibid.

30 Kevin Turner, personal communication with the author, December 14, 2012.

30 *New York Times*, "Carter Fast Recovering."

31 Theodore Roosevelt, *Presidential Addresses and State Papers*.

31 *Harvard Current*, "Physical Side of Football."

32 Reid and Smith, 308.

32 *Harvard Current*, "Physical Side of Football."

35 Leonard Shapiro, "The Hit That Changed a Career," *Washington Post*, November 18, 2005.

36 *Chicago Tribune*, ". . . But Mcmahon Still Walking Tall." October 12, 1988.

38 Robert C. Cantu and Mark Hyman, *Concussions and Our Kids: America's Leading Expert on How to Protect Young Athletes and Keep Sports Safe.* Boston: Houghton Mifflin Harcourt, 2012, 5.

42 Kevin Turner, personal communication with the author, December 14, 2012.

43 Trotter, Jim, "Don't Question Cutler's Toughness," *SI.com*, January, 23, 2011, http://sportsillustrated.cnn.com/2011/ writers/jim_trotter/01/23/packers .bears/ index.html (March 8, 2013).

44 *American Man*, produced and directed by Jon Frankel, 2012, available online at http://www. americanmanthemovie .com (March 19, 2013).

45 Cantu and Hyman, 83.

49 Steven Broglio, James T. Eckner, Douglas Martini, Jacob J. Sosnoff, Jeffrey S. Kutcher, and Christopher Randolf, "Cummulative Head Impact Burden in High School Football," *Journal of Neurotrauma* 28, no. 10 (2011): 2,074.

52 Shankar Vedantam, "Football Concussions and Brain Damage, from High School to the NFL." *Slate Magazine*, January 18, 2011, http://www.slate.com/articles/health_and_science/the_hidden_brain/2011/01/the_national_braindamage_league.html (August 21, 2012).

54 Emil Venere, "Brain Changes Found in Football Players Thought to Be Concussion-Free," Purdue University, October 7, 2010, http://www.purdue.edu/newsroom/research/2010/101007NaumanFootball.html (August 7, 2012).

54 GE Healthcare, "Blows to the Brain: Insight from Tragedy," *Signa Pulse*, Autumn 2010, 64–67.

54 Venere.

54 Vedantam.

55 Venere.

56 Pop Warner, "Rule Changes Regarding Practice & Concussion Prevention," *Pop Warner News Page*, n.d., http://www.popwarner.com/About_Us/Pop_Warner_News/Rule_Changes_Regarding_Practice___Concussion_Prevention_s1_p3977.htm (July 14, 2012).

57 Harrison S. Martland, "Punch Drunk," *Journal of the American Medical Association* 91, no. 15 (1928): 1,103–1,107.

58 Chris Nowinski, "Professional Wrestling Career," *Chris Nowinski Page*, n.d., http://www.chrisnowinski.com/ (November 13, 2012).

59 Christopher Nowinski, *Head Games*, Bridgewater, MA: Drummond Publishing Group, 2007, 2.

65 Mark Kram, "Deadly Aftershocks," *Philadelphia Daily News*, May 28, 2009, available online at http://www.sportsconcussion.com/pdf/misc/Aftershocks.pdf (March 25, 2013).

65–66 Alan Schwartz, "New Sign of Brain Damage in N.F.L.," *New York Times*, January 27, 2009.

66 Kram.

66 Lisa McHale, personal communication with the author, November 27, 2012.

67 Kevin Turner, personal communication with the author, December 14, 2012.

68 Lisa Horne, "ALS or Victim of Violent Sport?" *Fox Sports*, February 10, 2012, http://msn.foxsports.com/nfl/story/kevin-turner-former-college-and-nfl-running-back-battles-als-amyotrophic-lateral-sclerosis-lou-gehrig-disease-021012 (March 15, 2013).

68 Ibid.

70 Ibid.

70 "Kevin Turner (NFL)," Elite Talent Agency, n.d., http://www.eta-live.com/clients/detail/kevin_turner_nfl (January 18, 2013).

70 "Ex-Eagle Kevin Turner Has ALS," *Philly.com*, August 23, 2010, http://articles.philly.com/2010-08-23/sports/24972693_1_als-eagles-medical-study (March 13, 2013)

70 "Kevin Turner (NFL)."

72 Ron Stiles and Connie Stiles, personal communication with the author, December 3, 2012.

72 Wayne Drehs, "Nathan Stiles Wanted to Keep Playing," *ESPN*, November 28, 2010, http://sports.espn.go.com/espn/otl/news/story?id=5818575 (March 15, 2012).

73 Ron Stiles and Connie Stiles, personal communication.

74 Ibid.

74 Drehs.

74 Laura Bauer, "A Matter of Faith," *Kansas City Star*, May 15, 2011.

76 Ron Stiles and Connie Stiles, personal communication.

76 Nadia Kounang, "Brain Bank Examines Athletes' Hard Hits," *CNN Health*, January 27, 2012, http://www.cnn.com/2012/01/27/health/big-hits-broken-dreams-brain-bank (March 18, 2013)

76 Ron Stiles and Connie Stiles, personal communication.

77 Robert Cantu, "Dr. Robert Cantu Speaks Out about Concussions in Youth Sports," *SportsLetter*, October 1, 2012, http://www.sportsletter.org/sportsletter/2012/10/sl-interview-dr-robert-cantu-speaks-out-about-concussions-in-youth-sports.html (October 29, 2012).

78 Ann McKee, Robert Cantu, Christopher Nowinski, Tessa Hedley-Whyte, Brandon Gavett, Andrew Budson, Veronica Santini, Hyo-Soon Lee, Caroline Kubilus, and Robert Stern. "Chronic Traumatic Encephalopathy in Athletes: Progressive Tauopathy following Repetitive Head Injury." *National Institute of Health* 68, July 2009, 709-735.

79 Cantu and Hyman, 12.

79 Sports Legacy Institue, "Hit Count" White Paper," Sports Legacy Institute, February 3, 2012, n.d., http://www.sportslegacy.org/wp-content/uploads/2012/02/Hit-Count-White-Paper-FINAL-052512.pdf (March 13, 2013).

79 Sports Legacy Institue, "Sports Legacy Institute Announces Bold 'Hit Count' Initiative to Protect Youth Athletes through Regulating Brain Trauma Exposure," Sports Legacy Institute, February 3, 2012, http://www.sportslegacy.org/wp-content/uploads/2012/02/Hit-Count-Press-Release-FINAL020312-1.pdf (March 13, 2013).

80 Scott Powers, "Illinois Athletes Partake in Concussion Survey," *ESPNChicago*, December, 27, 2010, http://espn.go.com/blog/chicago/high-school/post/_/id/764/illinois-athletes-partake-in-concussion-survey (January 23, 2013).

80 Ibid.

84 Joan Pelly, personal communication with the author, March 6, 2013.

SELECTED BIBLIOGRAPHY

INTERVIEWS

Broglio, Steven P. Interview with the author, December 3, 2012.

Cantu, Robert. Interview with the author, March 25, 2013.

Kemp, Jeff. Interview with the author, January 29, 2013.

Leverenz, Larry. Interview with the author, August 23, 2012.

McHale, Lisa. Interview with the author, November 26, 2012.

McKee, Ann. Interview with the author, April 11, 2012.

Nauman, Eric. Interview with the author, August 23, 2012.

Pelly, Joan. Interview with the author, Personal interview. March 6, 2013.

Stiles, Ron and Connie. Interview with the author, December 3, 2012.

Talavage, Thomas. Interview with the author, August 23, 2012.

Turner, Kevin. Interview with the author, December 14, 2012.

OTHER SOURCES

Austin, Michael W., ed. *Football and Philosophy Going Deep.* Lexington: University Press of Kentucky, 2008.

Battey, George Magruder, Jr. "Anecdotes and Reminscences." In *A History of Rome and Floyd County.* Atlanta: Webb and Vary Company, 1922, 343–348. Google eBook, available online at http://books .google.com/books/about/A_History _of_Rome_and_Floyd_County_State .ntml?id=xvbTT88nRmoC (November 19, 2012).

Bauer, Laura. "A Matter of Faith." *Kansas City Star,* May 15, 2011.

Breedlove, Evan L., Meghan Robinson, Thomas M. Talavage, Katherine E. Morigaki, Umit Yoruk, Kyle O'Keefe, Jeff King, Larry J. Leverenz, Jeffrey W. Gilger, and Eric A. Nauman. "Biomechanical Correlates of Symptomatic and Asymptomatic Neurophysiological Impairment in High School Football." *Journal of Biomechanics* 45 (2012): 1,265–1,272.

Broglio, Steven P., James T. Eckner, Douglas Martini, Jacob J. Sosnoff, Jeffrey S. Kutcher, and Christopher Randolf. "Cumulative Head Impact Burden in High School Football." *Journal of Neurotrauma* 28, no. 10 (2011): 2,069–2,078.

Broglio, Steven P., Jacob J. Sosnoff, SungHoon Shin, Xuming He, Christopher Alcaraz, and Jerrad Zimmerman. "Head Impacts during High School Football: A Biomechanical Assessment." *Journal of Athletic Training* 44, no. 4 (July–August 2009): 342–349.

Cantu, Robert. "SL Interview: Dr. Robert Cantu Speaks Out about Concussions in Youth Sports." *SportsLetter.* October, 2012. http://www.sportsletter.org /sportsletter/2012/10/sl-interview- dr-robert-cantu-speaks-out-about- concussions-in-youth-sports.html (October 29, 2012).

Cantu, Robert C., and Mark Hyman. *Concussions and Our Kids: America's Leading Expert on How to Protect Young Athletes and Keep Sports Safe.* Boston: Houghton Mifflin Harcourt, 2012.

CDC. "Nonfatal Traumatic Brain Injuries Related to Sports and Recreation Activities among Persons Aged <= 19 Years United States, 2001–2009." *Centers for Disease Control and Prevention* 60, no. 39, 1,337–1,342. October 7, 2011. http://www .cdc.gov/mmwr/preview/mmwrhtml /mm6039a1.htm?s_cid=mm6039a1_w (April 5, 2012).

Daniel, Ray W. "Head Impact Exposure in Youth Football." *Annals of Biomedical Engineering,* February 15, 2012. http:// www.ncbi.nlm.nih.gov/pmc/articles /PMC3310979/ (April 5, 2012).

Daniloff, Caleb. "The Hardest Hit: Pro Athletes Are Donating Their Brains to BU for a Study of the Lasting Effects of Concussion." *Bostonia,* Winter 2008–2009. N.d. http://www.bu.edu/bostonia /winter09/concussions/ (June 20, 2012).

Doughterty, Jim, and Brandon Castel. *Survival Guide for Coaching Youth Football.* Champaign, IL: Human Kinetics, 2010.

Drehs, Wayne. "Nathan Stiles Wanted to Keep Playing." ESPN. November 28, 2010. http://sports.espn.go.com/espn/otl/news /story?id=5818575 (March 15, 2012).

Epstein, David. "The Damage Done." *Sports Illustrated*, November 2010, 42–45.

GE Healthcare. "Blows to the Brain: Insight from Tragedy." *Signa Pulse,* Autumn 2010, 64–67.

Gupta, Sanjay. "New Study Shows Head Injury Danger." *CNN.* June 22, 2011. http://www.cnn.com/video/#/video /bestoftv/2011/06/22/exp.am.gupta .concussion4.cnn?iref=videosearch (March 25, 2013).

Guskiewicz, K. M., S. W. Marshall, J. Bailes, M. McCrea, H. P. Harding, A. Matthews, J. R. Mihalik, and R. C. Cantu. "Recurrent Concussion and Risk of Depression in Retired Professional Football Players." *Medicine & Science in Sports & Exercise* 39, no. 6 (June 2007): 903–909.

Harvard Crimson. "Physical Side of Football." January 5, 1906. 2013. http:// www.thecrimson.com/article/1906/1/5 /physical-side-of-football-pthe-current/ (March 14, 2013).

Horne, Lisa. "Former College and NFL Running Back Kevin Turner Battles Amyotrophic Lateral Sclerosis, Also Known as Lou Gehrig Disease." *Fox Sports.* February 1, 2012. http://msn.foxsports .com/nfl/story/kevin-turner-former -college-and-nfl-running-back-battles -als-amyotrophic-lateral-sclerosis-lou -gehrig-disease-021012 (March 15, 2013).

Intelligence Squared U.S. Foundation. *Debate: Ban College Football.* Directed by John Donovan. Debaters Malcomb Gladwell, Buzz Bissinger, Tim Green, and Jason Whitlock. 2012. Available online at http://fora.tv/2012/05/08/Ban_College_ Football (October 26, 2012).

Israel, Michael. "Awareness and Attitudes of High School Athletes towards Concussions." American Academy of Pediatrics. October 22, 2012. https://aap .confex.com/aap/2012/webprogrampress /Paper15737.html (January 19, 2013).

Kaye, Ivan N. *Good Clean Violence: A History of College Football.* Philadelphia: J. B. Lippincott, 1973.

"Kevin Turner (NFL)." Elite Talent Agency. N.d. http://www.eta-live.com/clients /detail/kevin_turner_nfl/ (January 18, 2013).

Kram, Mark. "Deadly Aftershocks." *Phill.com.* May 28, 2009. 2012. http:// www.sportsconcussion.com/pdf/misc /Aftershocks.pdf (September 15, 2012).

Kounang, Nadia. "Brain Bank Examines Athletes' Hard Hits." CNN Health. January 27, 2012. http://www.cnn.com/2012/01/27 /health/big-hits-broken-dreams-brain- bank (March 18, 2013)

Langlois, Jean A., Wesley Rutland-Brown, and Marlena M. Wald. "The Epidemiology and Impact of Traumatic Brain Injury." *Journal of Head Trauma Rehabilitation* 21, no. 5 (2006): 375–378.

Lehman, Everett J., Misty J. Hein, Sherry L. Baron, and Christine M. Gersic. "Neurodegenerative Causes of Death among Retired National Football League Players." *Neurology* 79, no.19 (2012): 1,970–1,974.

Marar, Mallika, Natalie M. McIlvain, Sarah K. Fields, and R. Dawn Comstock. "Epidemiology of Concussions among United States High School Athletes in 20 Sports." *Ameican Journal of Sports Medicine* 40, no. 4 (January 27, 2012).

Martland, Harrison S. "Punch Drunk." *Journal of the American Medical Association* 91, no. 15 (1928): 1,103–1,107.

McCrory, P., W. Meeuwisse, K. Johnson, J. Dvorak, M. Aubry, M. Molloy, and R. Cantu. "Consensus Statement on Concussion in Sport: The 3rd International Conference on Concussion in Sport held in Zurich, November 2008." *British Journal of Sports Medicine* 43, Supplement 1 (2009): i76–i84.

McKee, Ann. Written testimony, hearing before the House Judiciary Committee, Legal Issues Relating to Football Head Injuries, October 28, 2009.

McKee, Ann, Robert Cantu, Christopher Nowinski, Tessa Hedley-Whyte, Brandon Gavett, Andrew Budson, Veronica Santini, Hyo-Soon Lee, Caroline Kubilus, and Robert Stern. "Chronic Traumatic Encephalopathy in Athletes: Progressive Tauopathy following Repetitive Head Injury." *National Institute of Health* 68 (July 2009): 709–735.

Meehan, William P. *Kids, Sports, and Concussion: A Guide for Coaches and Parents.* Santa Barbara, CA: Praeger, 2011.

Miller, Johnny. "Ronnie Lott Stunned by Loss of Fingertip." *SFGate*, July 31, 2011. http://www.sfgate.com/entertainment /article/Ronnie-Lott-stunned-by-loss-of- fingertip-1986-2352531.php (March 15, 2013).

Morris, Edmund. *Theodore Rex.* New York: Random House, 2001.

Mueller, Frederick O., and Robert C. Cantu. "Annual Survey of Catastrophic Football Injuries." *Annual Survey of Catastrophic Football Injuries.* N.d. http://www.unc .edu/depts/nccsi/FBCATReport2011.pdf (October 22, 2012).

Nowinski, Christopher. *Head Games.* Bridgewater, MA: Drummond Publishing Group, 2007.

Patoski, Joe Nick. *Texas High School Football: More Than the Game.* Austin: Bob Bullock Texas State History Museum, 2011.

PBS. "A Hard-Hitting Story: Young Football Players Take Big-League Hits to Head." *PBS.* N.d. http://www.pbs.org/newshour /bb/health/jan-june12/footballhits_04-02 .html (January 17, 2013).

Peterson, Robert W. *Pigskin: The Early Years of Pro Football.* New York: Oxford University Press, 1997.

Powers, Scott. "Illinois Athletes Partake in Concussion Survey—Chicago High School Blog." *ESPN.* N.d. http://espn.go.com/blog /chicago/high-school/post/_/id/764/illinois -athletes-partake-in-concussion-survey (January 23, 2013).

Purdue University, "Neuroimaging for Better Detection and Characterization of Brain Injuries." Information sheet. June 30, 2010.

Reid, Bill, and Ronald A. Smith. *Big-Time Football at Harvard, 1905: The Diary of Coach Bill Reid.* Urbana: University of Illinois Press, 1994.

Roosevelt, Theodore. Letter to Kermit Roosevelt, September 27, 1905. Theodore Roosevelt Collection. MS Am 1541 (121). Houghton Library, Harvard University. Available online at Theodore Roosevelt Digital Library. Dickinson State University. http://www.theodorerooseveltcenter .org/Research/Digital-Library/Record .aspx?libID=o280670 (March 25, 2013).

———. Letter to Kermit Roosevelt, November 1, 1905. Theodore Roosevelt Collection. MS Am 1541 (127). Houghton Library, Harvard University. Available online at Theodore Roosevelt Digital Library. Dickinson State University. http://www.theodorerooseveltcenter .org/Research/Digital-Library/Record .aspx?libID=o280676 (March 25, 2013).

———. *Theodore Roosevelt's Letters to His Children.* Edited by Joseph Bucklin Bishop. New York: Scribner's, 1919.

Segura, Melissa. "The Other Half of the Story." *Sports Illustrated Vault,* September 10, 2012. SI.com. Available online at http:// sportsillustrated.cnn.com/vault/article /magazine/MAG1205982/index.htm (March 14, 2013).

Stern, Robert, David O. Riley, Daniel H. Daneshvar, Christopher J. Nowinski, Robert C. Cantu, and Ann C. McKee. "Long-Term Consequences of Repetitive Brain Trauma: Chronic Traumatic Encephalopathy." *American Academy of Physical Medicine and Rehabilitation* 3 (October 2011): S460–S467. Available online at http://www.bu.edu/cste/files /2011/11/Stern-et-al-2011-PMR-Long- term-Consequences-of-Repetitive-Brain- Trauma1.pdf (January 18, 2013).

Talavage, Thomas M., Eric Nauman, Evan Breedlove, Umit Yoruk, Anne E. Dye, Katie Morigaki, Henry Feuer, and Larry Leverenz. "Functionally Detected Cogntive Impairment in High School Football Players without Clinically Diagnosed Concussion." *Journal of Neurotrauma,* October 1, 2010. 2012. Available online at http://online.liebertpub.com/doi/pdf /10.1089/neu.2010.1512 (August 16, 2012).

Trotter, Jim. "Don't Question Cutler's Toughness." *SI.com,* January 23, 2011. http://sportsillustrated.cnn.com/2011 /writers/jim_trotter/01/23/packers.bears /index.html#ixzz1BveiJewj (March 8, 2013).

"USA Football Overview." USA Football. N.d. http://usafootball.com/sites/default /files/USA_Football_one_pager_Dec_2010 .pdf. (March 15, 2013.)

Vedantam, Shankar. "The National Brain- Damage League: The Epidemic of Head Injuries in Football Is Even Worse Than You Thought." *Slate Magazine.* January 18, 2011. Available online at http://www .slate.com/articles/health_and_science /the_hidden_brain/2011/01/the_national _braindamage_league.html (August 21, 2012).

Venere, Emil. "Brain Changes Found in Football Players Thought to Be Concussion-Free." Purdue University. October 7, 2010. http://www.purdue.edu /newsroom/research/2010/101007Nauman Football.html (August 7, 2012).

Waterson, John Sayle. *College Football: History, Spectacle, Controversy.* Baltimore: John Hopkins University Press, 2000.

Zhao, L., W. Han, and C. Steiner. *Sports Related Concussions,* 2008. HCUP Statistical Brief #114. May 2011. Agency for Healthcare Research and Quality, Rockville, MD. http://www.hcup-us.ahrq .gov/reports/statbriefs/sb114.pdf (April 9, 2012).

FURTHER READING

BOOKS

Markle, Sandra. *Wounded Brains: True Survival Stories.* (Minneapolis: Lerner Publications Company, 2011).

Stewart, Mark, and Mike Kennedy. *Touchdown: The Power and Precision of Football's Perfect Play.* (Minneapolis: Millbrook Press, 2010).

WEBSITES

Center for Disease Control, Concussion in Sports:
http://www.cdc.gov/concussion/sports/index.html

Free online training course in concussion:
http://www.cdc.gov/concussion/HeadsUp/online_training.html

For free educational materials about concussions from the CDC:
www.cdc.gov/Concussion

To order free materials on concussions from the CDC:
http://wwwn.cdc.gov/pubs/ncipc.aspx#tbi1

To read the stories of concussion survivors:
http://www.cdc.gov/concussion/sports/stories.html

The Center of Excellence for Medical Multimedia has an interactive website that explains the anatomy and function of the brain:
http://www.traumaticbraininjuryatoz.org/The-Brain.aspx

Taylor Twellman, retired professional soccer player, has a web site to raise awareness of TBI:
http://www.thinktaylor.org

Web site to support awareness of concussions by former hockey players Keith Primeau and Kerry Goulet:
http://www.stopconcussions.com/

The Kevin Turner Foundation:
http://www.kevinturnerfoundation.org/

The Nathan Project:
http://www.nathanproject.com/

Eric Pelly Sports Education Fund:
http://www.ericpelly88.com/

RESOURCES FOR FEMALE ATHLETES

This book is about concussions in football. And since the game is primarily played by males, I wrote primarily about males. This is not intended in any way to ignore or minimize concussions experienced by females or the risk of concussions for millions of female athletes. Concussion is a serious issue for all people, regardless of gender.

An interview with Dr. Robert Cantu about the particular problem of concussions among female athletes:
http://www.momsteam.com/health-safety/concussions-women-more-succeptible

A TV-news feature on concussion in girls' soccer, including an interview with Cantu:
http://rockcenter.nbcnews.com/_news/2012/05/09/11604307-concussion-crisis-growing-in-girls-soccer

A TV-news feature on concussions in girls' hockey, including an interview with Dr. Dawn Comstock:
http://www.cbc.ca/player/undefined/ID/2147550291/

A *New York Times* article by Alan Schwarz detailing the problems of concussion diagnosis in girls' sports:
http://www.nytimes.com/2007/10/02/sports/othersports/02concussions.html

INDEX

ACKNOWLEDGMENTS

I want to thank my editor, Andrew Karre, for suggesting this book to me. It doesn't usually happen that way. Andrew knew this book was a good fit for me long before I did. He is a brilliant editor who sees both the big picture and the small details at the same time.

A book like this requires a lot of research, and I'm grateful to each person who shared their expertise with me and answered my countless questions.

My deepest appreciation goes to Ron and Connie Stiles (Nathan Stiles's parents), Joan Pelly (Eric Pelly's mother), and Lisa McHale (Tom McHale's wife). Each one shared the lives and deaths of their loved ones with me. Thank you for the photographs, information, and for trusting me to write about them.

I'm grateful to Kevin Turner, retired NFL player, for sharing his love of the game with me. With his special brand of honesty and humor, Kevin's stories gave me a glimpse into the world of football and how it feels to be a football player. I also appreciate Myra Turner, Kevin's mother, who shared his photographs with me.

My special thanks go to Dr. Ann McKee, neuropathologist at the Center for the Study of Traumatic Encephalopathy (CSTE). Dr. McKee shared images with me and graciously answered my questions so that I could better understand CTE in order to write about it. I am grateful to Dr. Robert Cantu for discussing his work with me. I'd also like to thank Sydney Wojtowicz at the CSTE, who provided me with information when I needed it and helped me in many different ways.

I am grateful to the researchers who shared their groundbreaking studies with me and answered my questions. Dr. Larry J. Leverenz, Dr. Thomas M. Talavage, and Dr. Eric A. Nauman at the Purdue Neurotrauma Group (PNG), Purdue University, discussed their work with me at length and generously shared their images. Dr. Steven Broglio, director of the Neurotrauma Research Laboratory at the University of Michigan, shared his research and helped me understand the scientific details.

Many others shared information with me for which I am grateful: Chris Nowinski, co-director of the CSTE and co-founder of the Sports Legacy Institute; Dr. Dawn Comstock, Ohio State University; Jeff Kemp, retired NFL player; Bob Colgate, Director of Sports and Sports Medicine for the National Federation of State High School Associations (NFHS); Joey Walters, Arkansas Activities Association; Jason Cates, President of the Arkansas Association of Athletic Trainers; Dr. Darrell Nesmith, Adolescent Medicine at Arkansas Children's Hospital; Darrell Ellis, offensive coordinator at Glen Rose High School, Malvern, Arkansas. A special thank-you goes to Christa Finney (athletic trainer), Mike Lee (athletic director) and Paul Calley (head coach) at Bryant High School in Bryant, Arkansas. They answered my questions, let me watch them at work, and allowed me to stand on the sideline during a home football game.

ABOUT THE AUTHOR

Carla Killough McClafferty is the author of a number of award-winning books for young readers, including *The Many Faces of George Washington: Remaking a Presidential Icon*, *Something Out of Nothing: Marie Curie and Radium*, and *In Defiance of Hitler: The Secret Mission of Varian Fry*. Before becoming an author, McClafferty worked as a registered radiologic technologist. She lives in Benton, Arkansas. Visit her online at www.carlamcclafferty.com.

PHOTO ACKNOWLEDGMENTS

The images in this book are used with the permission of: © iStockphoto.com/Kittiyut Phornphibul, (grass); © Provided by the University of Georgia Athletic Association, pp. 9 (both); Walter Chauncey Camp papers, 1870–1983 (inclusive), 1870–1925 (bulk). Manuscripts and Archives, Yale University Library, p. 10; Yale Athletics Photographs ca. 1850–2007 (inclusive). Manuscripts and Archives, Yale University Library, p. 11; Library of Congress pp. 12, 13, (LC-USZ62-132674); 15, (LC-DIG-ppmsca-25994); 18, (LC-USZ62-8665); 22, (LC-USZ62-125359); SDN-004530, Chicago Daily News negatives collection/Chicago History Museum, p. 13 (inset); © Harvard Varsity football squad: Harvard University Archives, HUPSF Football (160), p. 19; © Illegal football move: Harvard University Archives, HUPSF Football (119), p. 25; Courtesy of the Turner family, pp. 30, 68; AP Photo/Butch Dill, p. 32 (left); © Mark Kauffman/Time & Life Pictures/Getty Images, p. 32 (right); © Evan Oto/Photo Researchers, Inc., p. 34; Amie Sachs/CNP/Newscom, p. 36; © Laura Westlund/Independent Picture Service, p. 39; Photo by Vernon Doucette for Boston University Photography, p. 40; © Focus on Sport/Getty Images, p. 43; © Riddell, p. 47 (both); © Purdue University, pp. 50, 51, 52; Purdue University image/Thomas Talavage, p. 53; © George Gojkovich/Getty Images, p. 58; © Jennifer Pottheiser/Getty Images, p. 59; © Stan Grossfield/The Boston Globe/Getty Images, p. 61; © Ann C. McKee, MD/VA Boston HealthCare System/Boston University School of Medicine, pp. 63 (both), 85; Courtesy of the McHale Family, pp. 65, 66; © Ezra O. Shaw/Allsport/Getty Images, p. 69; Courtesy of Tim Carroll, pp. 72, 73, 74, 75; Courtesy of the Pelly family, p. 83.

Front cover: AP Photo/Alex Brandon (main); © iStockphoto.com/Kittiyut Phornphibul, (grass). Back cover: © Yobro10/Dreamstime.com.